To Brian,
Please enjoy this gift.

CLOSE YOUR EYES TO FIND YOUR WAY

CLOSE YOUR EYES TO FIND YOUR WAY

A Guide to Discovering Your Higher Self

JEFFREY B. BRANDT

COPYRIGHT © 2009 BY JEFFREY B. BRANDT.

LIBRARY OF CONGRESS CONTROL NUMBER: 2009901076
ISBN: HARDCOVER 978-1-4415-0976-5
SOFTCOVER 978-1-4415-0975-8

All rights reserved. No part of this book may be reproduced or transmitted in any form or by any means, electronic or mechanical, including photocopying, recording, or by any information storage and retrieval system, without permission in writing from the copyright owner.

This book was printed in the United States of America.

To order additional copies of this book, contact:
Xlibris Corporation
1-888-795-4274
www.Xlibris.com
Orders@Xlibris.com
58119

CONTENTS

Introduction:	The Search to Find Your Way	11
	How This Book Is Different	15
Chapter I:	The Silent Witness	25
Chapter II:	The Garden of Eden	29
Chapter III:	History	37
Chapter IV:	Religion	53
Chapter V:	The Messiah's Life	57
Chapter VI:	Children Are the Teachers	65
	Life stages	67
Chapter VII:	Prophecy	75
	Will vs. Imagination	77
Chapter VIII:	Life Diversity	81
Chapter IX:	Dreaming	89
	Dreams and Memories	
Chapter X:	Success	95
Chapter XI:	Suffering	103
Chapter XII:	The Key: The Power of Energy	109
Chapter XIII:	The Journey	123
In Conclusion		131
Index		135

To Margarita and Naomi
My inspiration to be a better person

Get to know yourself, and you will come to know a miracle!

Introduction

THE SEARCH TO FIND YOUR WAY

We all, in our own way, seem to be searching for some elusive quality to life. It may be fame, fortune, success, security, love, personal satisfaction, purpose, or any of a dozen other ideals. Whatever it is we are looking for, the search itself seems to be inherent to the human condition from the time an infant discovers the world through innocent eyes or reaches out with curious hands. Later, as the child learns to walk, the search grows to ever expanding limits. This search often takes us into adulthood and beyond. For some, this search may never end as long as they are alive. Few are those who find themselves truly satisfied with their life situation.

The world seems eager to comply with this search as well. This is evident in the energy and resources invested in advertising with the proposition of bringing satisfaction to this insatiable hunger for something. We have come so far in our development. Yet the need for continuing this search seems to be greater than ever before.

We find countless organizations, programs, books, tapes, and videos promising to show us a better way to live. There is truth to many, if not all, of these methods. Yet many people who indulge themselves in taking them up continue to feel there is something more needed. Is this a bad thing, or does it necessarily signify failure of some sort on our part? I doubt it. In any case, the search itself does bring to each of us moments of revelation that do seem to satisfy us, at least for a while. And this is a good thing.

The more of these moments of revelation that are revealed to us, the more we grow in our own right. Many have experienced already enough of these moments of revelation to be ready to cement them together. In doing so, they may find a lasting satisfaction which will give them the ability to maintain throughout the inevitable trials and tribulations of life and the opportunity to share with others a better way. This is where I see the majority of us in this time of human history.

The world is a paradox. We can now see more evil and wicked deeds than at any other time in history. At the same time, however, we can see more hope for a beautiful new beginning than at any time previous to ours. It all seems to be a matter of perspective, of personal choice. It is as if the whole of human history has been dedicated to the building of two very separate yet parallel roads. One is built on the premise of fear and the other on the premise of love. Let this humble quest be one more brick to pave the way on our evolutionary path toward helping the latter reign triumphant.

I don't believe in mere coincidence without a higher purpose. You picked up this book for a reason. Although it may not have all of the answers you seek, I believe it is what you need to see at this moment in your life. I believe it is important to realize that life tends to work out in this way.

We tend to come across exactly the things that we need at just the right time in order for us to grow personally. The key is to recognize this because often what we come across is not so pleasant, but it is always something necessary to help us identify and achieve our higher purpose. Once recognized as something necessary, we may alter our perspective of the most difficult situations we face in our life and maybe even welcome them. This would be the ideal.

The intensity of our desire to continue in this search seems to be in direct correlation with just how much pain we are experiencing in any given moment. In other words, the more pain one experiences, the more one feels compelled to search for deeper meaning to the pain being experienced. When we feel physical hunger, we seek food; although, it is not the food in its original form that we actually use. A carrot, for example, is good for the eyes. But you will not find carrots in the eyes. We must first ingest it, digest it, and assimilate it. We use the nutrients from this food to build and better our vision, and that which remains is then discarded.

The same is with knowledge, our spiritual food. When we hunger for answers, we seek knowledge; but we don't use this knowledge in its original form. Like food, we need to first ingest it, digest it, and assimilate it. We may then discard that which we don't at that time need. The comparison is readily noted in the phrase "food for thought."

Let this book be a snack or a smorgasbord. Whatever you find it to be, I am confident that you will find in it exactly what you need at this moment in your life. Like with food, our hunger for knowledge will always return after a time of fasting. You will undoubtedly never find any one book to have within it all you will ever need in your quest for knowledge. It is therefore always recommended that we continually seek out further intellectual stimulation. For this reason, understand that a lifelong search is nothing abnormal. Rather it is the sign of a healthy mind, a growing mind. Let this be inspirational to you if you are one who feels compelled to continue this search until the end of your life.

I feel blessed by the experience of having written this book. At the same time, I must admit that it has been a most humbling experience. For all those who understand that state of mind that surges from somewhere deep inside of us at the moment of revelation, may you know that this final product, this book, was not the result of mere conscious thought or observation. It came from somewhere beyond myself. Hence, I cannot feel justified in taking credit for all that was written. This book was obviously influenced by other books I have read over the years by numerous other writers; however, I sense something very unique about the way this book has turned out. Oftentimes, during the process of writing this book, I felt genuinely excited to see just where it was taking me. It was as if I were only going along for the ride, so to speak.

In writing this book, I was not only trying to explain what it is we are searching for. I myself was on that very same search, and I did not know with any great clarity what that something was either. In this respect, the writing experience, for me, was a learning experience as much as it was a teaching experience. This is how I believe the best of teaching is practiced. The best teachers are also the best students. They are the best because they are not above learning alongside their pupils, even learning from the very lesson they are presently teaching those pupils.

It is true then, that we are all students of life. We are all teachers as well. We are on this journey together, and that is how it should be. We play each role to the best of our ability, and all benefit who are involved in the search whether they be teacher or student in any given moment. We are here to share and to grow together.

I have given the very best of myself in writing this book and sincerely hope you find within it your own key to a better way, a way that you truly deserve to find. Anyone who embarks upon the journey to self-discovery knows this journey may be a tortuous one. However, its commencement is not always voluntary; and once begun, it becomes a journey with no return.

As birth is the way into this world and death the way into the next, the search is the way to bring our worlds together. Birth and death are both moments of transition. Transition is often painful. Once transition is complete, the pain is forgotten; and we discover new and better things. Keep this in mind throughout your personal journey of transition, and always do your very best to allow the inevitable to happen. Work with your journey, not against it. And your journey will be much more pleasant.

The proposition of this book is to help you through this transition, to ease you into your own state of self-discovery, to be of aid to you in cementing your own moments of revelation, and to create within you the correct mindset to provide for a lasting satisfaction that endures through whatever life throws into your path. Suffering, although it appears to be something unavoidable for all who have embarked upon the journey of self-discovery or enlightenment, and I have been not spared this same suffering, I believe is not an absolute necessity. I do not see it as something we really need to be concerned with so much as how we are growing in our own right. The principal element of concern should rather be on our growth. Accept the suffering if and when it comes by knowing you are in good company.

How This Book Is Different

If there is one aspect of this book that sets it apart from the numerous other books on the topic of self-realization, it would be in the approach it takes to present this search. Most books on this topic—including this book—will tell you the answers you seek can be found within you. This is where the similarity ends. Where most books go on to explain how we can raise our spiritual awareness, they cite what so many maestros from different disciplines have expressed concerning said matter.

Yes, this book makes few references of this sort as well; however, I have tried to minimize this. I feel its effect on the overall goal is minimal.

Many of these references we've heard before, and they may be meaningful to us at the moment but not necessarily something we will carry with us. We remember having heard or read them somewhere else, but they likely didn't impact us enough to memorize them. This is because they are words. Words are in the realm of the mind. They can impact the mind but continue to fail in helping us connect to the spirit.

What we seek is a connection with the spirit; and the truth is our spirit, on its most essential level, does not rely on language. Rather, the spirit relies on energy. Spirit is energy, pure and simple. Yes, words can be effective in the invocation of energy; but what truly invokes energy is raw awareness. Awareness arises from still observation. What do we observe most in life? We observe our world and our experiences, our thoughts, our reactions, and the actions and reactions of others. It is for this reason that I have relied on these elements to convey the meaning of the message and avoided the use of outside word references as much as possible.

It may be said that without citing specific references to outside word sources, this book lacks in credibility. This may or may not be true. It is an opinion. It all depends on what you consider to be a credible source. And, even then, it further depends on how you interpret that source. I will say that I have seen far too many books—some, very well-referenced, I might add—being torn apart by critics and used as fodder to ignite great violence. I wish to avoid this by stating that the entirety of this book is based solely on my humble perspective, my interpretation, my opinion, if you will.

It is not my intention to prove or disprove anything regarding the truth or nontruth of any of the ideas put forth in this book. My intention is to appeal to that inner knowing that I believe each one of us possess. Intuition, as this inner knowing is often called, is a function of our being that I believe our society has taught us to ignore over the generations.

I'm not referring to something esoteric here. Rather, I am referring to what we commonly experience as a simple hunch. Whether we decide to pay heed to these hunches may make a significant difference in how our lives play out.

The basic premise of this book is that we can find our way best by depending on our own voice. This would include in our interactions with others. I am a strong believer there is a very potent force in our midst that compels us to do the right thing and that our problems begin where we begin to veer from this guiding force in favor of what we have been taught by our society.

You will find in this book a combination of storytelling, thoughts to ponder, conversational language, and straight-up advice. The voice used imparts a human quality you don't find in the typical textbook approach. Nor do you feel the condescending voice of a spiritual master who seems to be writing from a monastery, out of touch with all of the trivialities of the "real" world which we must face on a daily basis.

One last point I would like to make before beginning the book is about religion. There are a great number of religions that have developed throughout the world that present answers to this search. Within the influence of every one of these religions, we can find individuals who for one reason or another continue to suffer in their personal search for meaning.

This search by its very nature is individual. Being individual, any outside influence is likely to be lacking. Whatever answers may be provided by any religion must somehow be internalized to have an effective result. There are individuals who we may consider to be truly enlightened by the influence of any one of these religions as well as there are those who are somehow left out.

JEFFREY B. BRANDT

It is not my intention to patronize or to condemn any particular religion in presenting my case. In fact, my feelings are neutral in regards to any religion. Obviously, my presentation expresses more of a Christian perspective. My own influence has been such. I grew up in the middle of the United States, where Christianity was about the only religious influence I experienced. My only knowledge of other religions came from the media, whether it was in the books I read, on the television, or at the movies. I did not know anyone who was not of the Christian persuasion while growing up.

Although my only firsthand religious influence was with Christianity, I must confess I was not a very good Christian. I grew up in a mostly conformist society, going to church every Sunday and becoming confirmed by the Lutheran church. However, I was very much drawn to history as a young child. What I saw historically did not sit well with me. I felt for the Indians who were indigenous to the area I grew up in. I felt their plight as their culture, which seemed to be so harmonious with their world, was destroyed by the arriving culture, one of Christians.

The more I learned of history, the more I saw how the culture of Christianity had basically destroyed every indigenous culture it came across as the Western culture grew to encompass new territory. It was for this reason that I began to look into other cultures and religions. I must also admit, I am not in any way an expert on religious affairs; but I don't see where being an expert is always helpful in such personal affairs. The essence, after all, of any religion is the same. It is about our purpose, the purpose of our lives and our world. This purpose is the same for any human being, independent from their religious influence.

This is where this book begins. Let it bring not separation but continuity to our common struggle. We are all on the same journey. We are all searching for the same answers. Let us focus on how much we have in common, and let the differences be just that. They are differences because no two lives are ever walked the same way, and this is not a bad thing.

Enjoy this book, and let me know how it has influenced your search. I welcome any and all correspondence and will do my best to respond to all those who wish.

When opening a new book,
we should also remember to open our mind.

Close Your Eyes to Find Your Way

Chapter I

THE SILENT WITNESS

Take a moment to look back over your life. Draw upon the mental images you have stored of all the significant moments of your past. Add a few of the not-so-significant moments, and play them back now like a movie of your life. The order is not so important. If you jump around a bit, that's OK. Feel each one of your memories, your moments of pride, and your regrets. There were surely challenges you have met and overcome, and there were others that defeated you. You have felt moments of acceptance that brought you joy and moments of abandonment that hurt. Dwell for a while on all you have done and all you have felt in your past. Make it as real as you possibly can and then close the door.

Turn around now, and face your future. See all of your hopes, dreams, and wishes for times yet to come. Think about the plans you have, and imagine how they will come out. Be honest if, perhaps, you feel a little uncertain about what may happen. Do you believe you will find total success, or will your future be a mix of success with some failures? Imagine every possible scenario. How do you imagine yourself a year from now, five years from now, twenty years from now? Think about it and then close the door.

JEFFREY B. BRANDT

Look at who you are now. Are you a man or a woman, an adult or a child? Are you married? Are you red, black, white, brown, or yellow? Are you tall or short, heavy or thin? Are you an American? Are you a doctor, a sales clerk, a waitress? Are you important? How about in the eyes of others? Are you in good health? Are you an ambitious go-getter or more laidback? Are you a religious person or an atheist? Close your eyes, and cover your ears.

Feel yourself in this moment. Are you happy? Are you lonely, confident, or scared? Do you feel comfortable with what you are reading? Do you feel curious at this moment? Or perhaps you feel excited. Think about how you feel right now and then extinguish your emotions.

What is left? Can you hear a voice from somewhere inside of you? Listen to what it says. Is it making some commentary relative to this little exercise? Perhaps you are wondering to where it is leading. Listen to the nature of this commentary for a moment. This voice you hear is your thought process. Notice how it seems to flit from one thought to another, sometimes in order and other times randomly. Notice how it tends to repeat itself quite frequently as well. Allow yourself to observe what it is saying for a while. Then ask yourself to whom this voice is directed.

It is directed to the silent witness. Who is this silent witness? It is you stripped of your past and your future. It is you without the many labels you carry along to identify yourself with. It is you beneath the emotion, the uncertainty, and the judgment. It is your truest self, your essential self. It is the same self which has remained virtually unchanged since the beginning of your life, this life. It is the self that can only say, "I am the silent witness. I am the here and the now. I am I, and I am you. I am always there, here, and everywhere." This is where you should be. Here you are the same as every man, woman, and child. Here you are the same as every saint and every sinner.

On the surface, we have so many different roles in life. We are like actors. We change our roles to suit the needs of the moment. In this moment, I am the father. Then my wife arrives, and I am the husband. I am happy until she tells me she's leaving me. I become sad or angry, or both. If I have a bad day, I become a bad person. If I'm feeling good, I become a nice person. Things can change from day to day or even in a moment. But this is only the surface of a stormy ocean. We can submerge to the depths of ourselves to find the calm that is always undaunted by the trivialities of life on the surface. Close the door.

This is the place I am in as I write this book, and this is the place where you should be as you read this book. Here is where we are one, no matter our nationality, the color of our skin, our social status, no matter the language we speak or the state of mind we find ourselves. We are one, and we are the same. Here, there is no fear. There is no unknown or uncertainty. If we dwell in this place for a time, we will begin to understand. Our revelation will begin. This is not hope. This, simply, is the nature of who we are.

In every major religion and philosophy, it speaks of the importance of the here and the now. The *here* refers to the place deep within each one of us, beneath the labels we use to identify ourselves and beneath the emotions, to the place our true self exists. In this place, there is no real separation from anything that exists. We are one with the world around us.

It is from this place that the message of this book begins, for the focus of improving our circumstance must always begin here to be truly effective. From this point, we are naturally in the present moment; the here and the now are both one and the same. The now means living in the present moment.

Chapter II

THE GARDEN OF EDEN

The Garden of Eden was considered a perfect place, a place in which man was meant to live forever in a state of perfection. Perfection cannot be destroyed by man. It is not mentioned that it was destroyed by God either. Mankind didn't destroy this garden, and God didn't destroy it. It is said that we had to leave this garden; so what happened to this Garden of Eden? Nothing happened to the garden. Where is it? Our concept of it being a place where we were once and are no longer is a misunderstood concept.

If we cannot return, it is because we are no longer able to see it for what it really is. Our eyes have become tainted by our apparent need to search for the perfection that we no longer sense in our existence. It still exists. It is everywhere and nowhere. It is never and forever. The garden remains as it has always been. It is we who no longer exist as we always have. It is we who have separated ourselves from this supposed place called the Garden of Eden.

We only sense that something is lacking. What we sense is an illusion. This is the essence of that which we call original sin. We sense a nakedness about ourselves, and we don't feel natural in our nakedness. We try to hide ourselves from all and even from ourselves. The supposed fig leaf represents just how little we actually disguise our essence in this attempt. We are but children before the grand scheme of things, before the eyes of God.

Adam may not have been a single man but a representation of mankind in his perfect state. We don't really know. His children, likewise, may have been merely representative of our continuing fall from this state of harmony with the world (the grace of God), which is perfect and always will be, everlasting. The act of Cain killing Abel could only represent the first intentional killing of another man.

This original perfection, although it has ceased to us, remains a part of us. No matter how small this part may seem. Our purpose is to find this part and to grow within it, leaving behind that which is flawed. We are what we are.

The world is perfect in its natural sense. It continues. It doesn't concern itself with the details of how it will continue. It simply continues. It is only what mankind has done within this world that lack perfection.

In our error, we have grown to consider that which we have created as the real world. We cannot destroy the real world; we can only destroy ourselves. By the same token, we cannot improve this world; we can only improve ourselves. This is the lesson this world has been teaching us all along and will continue to teach us. Even as we consume entire planets, if this be the case someday, we will never destroy our world. We must realize this. Don't worry about the world. It will be here long after you and I have departed from this plane. What we need to focus on is what we are doing to ourselves by way of what we believe we are doing to the world. We need to clear our vision.

We have accumulated an immense wealth of knowledge about our world. There was a time when man had to struggle against great odds just to survive. Inclement weather can be deadly without the modern structures we enjoy today. And there was always the threat of being killed by the local wildlife.

All of these natural dangers have long been overcome. Ways have been found to minimize or completely avoid their threat. In our ignorance, we have not yet realized this; or so it may seem. We have only replaced these threats with our own artificial threats. Today you cannot trust your neighbor's intentions. For this reason, we must protect ourselves with pages of laws and contracts and all that we call legalese. Even with all of this, we are still in danger from predators of our own species. We are the only species that will attack its own without even the slightest provocation. And we do so all too frequently. And for what purpose do we attack, I ask?

Surely, we have done wonders in this quest to improve our position in the world. We have made some truly awesome discoveries, and we have applied these discoveries in absolutely mind-boggling ways. I really see no wrongdoing in the ideas or even in the actions we take to this end in whatever form they may take. What saddens me is the thought of at what sense of urgency we place on our illusionary need to change our world. Who or what are we really serving here? If we are to continue advancing, to where shall we set our aim? Yes, we have improved our position in the world. But what is all of this worth when we have done at least as much to sabotage that same position?

We are at the point today where we can see perfectly well what effects many of our so-called advances have done and are doing in relation to our fellow beings and to our environment. Still, it seems to take litigation or some form of political pressure for us to alter our ways when what we do is known to be detrimental to us. And beyond this, we so often have the audacity to even fight this litigation or political pressure for the purpose of serving only our self-centered and shortsighted interests.

We may have no desire to return to living in the deserts, forests, and jungles as we once did in that primitive way. We have tasted a different life, and that is fine. Surely, there have been, are, and will be people who see returning to a more primitive way as the answer to our problems. And, yes, there are answers to be found on this path; but, as I said, the world will continue regardless of what we do. This tells us that in spite of all that we have done to our world, there is still hope to continue without resorting to such drastic and likely undesirable measures.

These are details of which the world doesn't concern itself. It is the essence of our ways that really needs to change. In improving our position in this world, we need to use our awareness of the effects of those changes. We have the technology to create fuels which don't pollute. We have the ability to live more in harmony with the creatures that share with us this planet. We have the means of using all of our precious resources more efficiently. Most importantly, it is a basic attitude about how we need to respect others and ourselves in our everyday dealings.

These are all concepts we have tried to deal with through litigation. This litigation has only created greater levels of the same mess. You see, in essence, nothing has changed here. One party is trying to control another party to keep that party from controlling something. In doing thus, we are only propagating more of the same. The answer doesn't lie out there. In trying to control another, we are sending the message that in essence nothing that the other party is doing is really wrong. We are saying that it is OK to try to control another. After all, we are doing it. They are merely fighting for the same thing we are—control.

If, for example, a company is destroying habitats, producing a product that is detrimental to our health, or simply being dishonest in its dealings, we have a choice to support that company or not to support it. If we try to force litigation, it will likely fight that litigation. Maybe with time we could close it down or convince it to change its ways. The same goes for trying to force customers away from that company through harassment or any other aggressive techniques. In either case, it is unlikely we will have done anything to cause a profound change in the heart of any other being. The story will continue, and the plot will thicken. Many companies today go to great lengths to deceive the world in their self-interests.

The bottom line for mostly every company is the dollar, not some idealistic company conscience we hear so much talk of these days. It is for this reason so much of the litigation aimed at controlling companies is founded on some sort of financial imposition. Laws that protect our environment or ourselves become weapons that can be used against us as well. Laws are not the fundamental answers we need to seek. If we seek any fundamental change, it must begin within ourselves.

If the bottom line is the dollar, don't support that company, period. If you wish other people to do the same, express this through your example. Express yourself, yes; but limit your expression to sharing yourself with others. Forcing your will upon them will only propagate that which you are fighting. The whole idea of believing that it's acceptable to force our will (because it is right) is misunderstood, and this has been proven again and again throughout history. Battles may be won, but we continue to lose the war. Don't make the error of treating the situation as a battle; it will become a war. You don't reap oranges when all you have sowed were apples.

If you want a better world, create a better world within yourself. Use your energies to propagate that which you would like to see in the world. Always begin within yourself. Who has influenced more people than anyone else in the entire history of our planet? It was a man who never lifted a sword, never wrote a book, and never held an office. He never did many of the things we tend to associate with power and influence. All he did was express himself through his perfect example. He lived what he wished us to live. And he invited us to do the same.

Perhaps you don't wish to live your life to this extreme as he did. That is fine. I tend to believe in a certain form that he suffered, probably, more than any other person ever has. But I would be willing to bet he was also more at peace with himself and his world than any other person who has ever lived. This seems a paradox, and it is. It is one that can only be truly understood through experience. Through this experience you will attain a vision of life that is totally clear and free from illusion of any kind. You will understand the meaning of life. And this is something every soul is capable of experiencing.

Transition Awareness

The realization of the meaning of life could be compared to stepping through a door into a new universe. The view of this new universe is as a mirror image of the old. Everything once familiar is now seen in an entirely new way. Everything that was not known or understood before becomes familiar, a twist of something already known. Everything in the universe becomes new and ancient at the same time. Time has been washed away, only to reveal itself in glimpses as eternity once did before.

This new universe holds promise beyond anything you have experienced. The promise is of a different sort than you would have expected previous to this transition. What was once considered monumental suddenly becomes trivial. And that which had little significance before becomes sacred. Along with this promise comes a nakedness, a nakedness of self and of all those around you. Illusion becomes, as time, nonexistent.

Once this step has been taken, there is no turning back. Any attempt at regression to a more naïve way is instantly recognized to be superficial only. The price of this attempt is a heavy burden of guilt, shame, and an almost unbearable pain. The reward for remaining true is equally opposite, an untouchable calm of the soul and a euphoric joy of the heart.

However subjective this universe may appear to those not experiencing themselves in this way, you find their arguments to be, as so many of their arguments, pointless and irrelevant. This is just another example of one of those monumental essences turned trivial.

Chapter III

History

Before there existed priests and politicians, it was the natural law that maintained humanity within the context of total harmony. There was no straying. In the most natural sense, we lived out our lives in the purity of uncontaminated innocence. The whole concept of sin was null as sin itself. Each man was responsible for himself and his. Anything beyond this simply wasn't contemplated. It wasn't recognized. And this experience of untainted innocence continued. Humanity thrived in a timeless continuum that knew nothing of guilt or sickness, the symptoms of sin. Mankind was perfect in a spiritual sense.

We were social creatures for sure, but we mostly limited our groups to immediate or extended families. These groups wandered, mostly without aim, hunting and gathering what they could to survive and to experience the grand simplicity of life.

From time to time, one band or family may have crossed paths with another; and surely there had been conflicts, the same as we can observe in any confrontation in the animal kingdom. Rare was the time that these confrontations would result in anything more serious than a frightening experience for either of the two parties involved. In the rare occasion where blood may have been spilled, it was quickly forgotten as one or the other party moved on. With these confrontations, the continuum was not broken or even weakened. It was an accepted part of the only existence that was known. Call it blissful ignorance if you will, but it was beautiful nonetheless.

With the dawn of civilization, we came to see the benefits of interdependence. For the first time, we began to specialize our life focus. We began to leave behind the ability to survive alone in exchange for what we surely perceived as something better. This was our first experience of breaking the circle. The idea was to make the lives of each more efficient. The reality is that we have done not much other than delude ourselves in this quest.

With this breaking of the circle, we had more time to contemplate things. We began to question what we had never before considered, life. Could it be more than living as we were? What we failed at was in asking about ourselves, our motivations for the change. As the children we were, we quickly forgot our recent past. Our change became not an experiment to be tested and evaluated with the idea of acceptance or rejection. Our sense of logic had not been developed to this degree as of yet.

Life itself became a search. How to do what we do better than we had done before? Suddenly, there came the concept that something could be lacking in our lives. We began to discover more efficient ways of doing everything. And with this came the question of how far we could take this idea of improvement. Logic then became a part of our thinking, and logic became our worst enemy.

The enemy, being within our collective psyche, was not noticed in our journey from innocence. Our focus had not yet turned inward. We continued to focus on the world around us, as this was the only world we knew and could observe. We had not yet realized our spiritual selves.

As time went along, there came hints meant to show us our error. Most continued to ignore these signs. A few did notice. These were the ones that conceived the idea of governing our groups. Of those that did, there were those whose ignorance continued to keep them blinded from what we held inside. They became the politicians. They placed their focus on controlling the external, our actions. The concept of law came to be.

A few were more insightful and placed their focus on what was internal to us. They became the priests. From them came the concept of morality. From the birth of morality came the first feelings of guilt. Hence, sickness became an intimate part of our existence. The first priests would also become our first doctors and therapists.

The vast majority remained ignorant to what was seen by the priests. Thus, what the priests intended to share was seen with awe. The concept of reverence was born. Priests held a special place within these early groups of people. It was perhaps from this awe they held that the ego first made its appearance. So began the countless rituals that have been performed and the beginning of symbolism. This was only natural, given the desire to ensure the continuance of the elevated status one could enjoy being a priest.

As ego became rooted, others began to consider and yearn for this special treatment. Principally, it was noted among the politicians. But it was also noted among the strong, who made their claim to whatever goods they deemed desirable. Envy had made its presence known. With envy established and fed by ego, greed was soon to follow. In an attempt to control the strong, the first police were designated. The concept of bad had been given birth.

The whole concept of humanity had been changed with the advent of envy and greed. We became not scavengers but predators. Violence became known to us. We had now completely severed the circle and became apart from the rest of our world. For the first time, we were alone. We no longer saw the earth as our mother. No more could we coexist with the animals. We categorized the plants either as useful resources or as weeds. We began to view the earth's resources as something of raw material to be reckoned with. We lost the innocence and the innate reverence which had been so much a part of our consciousness.

Violence had not existed before envy and greed, which are born of the ego. The concept of intentionally killing or even harming another or ourselves was not in us. By nature, we were peaceful, even fearful creatures. We viewed our world in awe. These qualities are not gone from our being. They have only been suppressed.

With this change began the struggle to survive. Life ceased to provide for us as it always had before, or so it seemed with our growing fear. This fear was caused by the awareness of our separation from all that was. What was once respected was now feared, and the incessant need to control our environment began to develop.

And so, history was born. Advances proved greater with every discovery. And with every advance, came the growing feeling of emptiness. The powers that existed in our environment were great, and it would be many thousands of years before we would learn to protect ourselves from this phenomenon. In fact, to this day, we have yet to be completely protected.

During these thousands of years, the confrontations we faced became greater in both number and magnitude. The signs meant to show us our error became increasingly noticeable also. The first prophets made their presence known. Over the next several thousand years, the land came to know several great mentors or messiahs. In essence, their messages were the same. In spite of this, there remained confusion on the part of the masses. The people continued to feel divided. Only now, they had only more reason to feel so. They had their various religions. Although the basic word of the messengers had been essentially the same in each case, it was the practice of the rituals created by the followers that muddled the pure and simple message. This was the beginning of the church.

The first holy wars were then begun. In these wars, we knew a vengeance like never before. The violence was elevated to unprecedented levels. Simple death was no longer sufficient. We had become aware of our spiritual side, and punishment had to address this issue. It was more than the body that had to become a victim. The spirit had to be broken or saved in our ignorance. Torture of another human being became the standard of the day.

With this new kind of war, new methods had to be developed. Brute strength was eventually found to be inferior to something new. This something new came to be known as technology. Technology came about with the purpose of war and control of whatever was foreign.

With the advent of technological advance came an even greater need for resources, more than could be had at hand. Humanity began to move like never before. No longer was he simply wandering aimlessly through the wilderness. His intention was to explore and conquer what lied before him. With the unprecedented aggression that developed, new means of transportation were created for people and goods.

This was the era of great civilizations and empires. They grew, and they died. With these great empires came the use of slaves to build them. And with the power held by the few, entertainment became known. Each time, the entertainment came more at the cost of others' lives with carnal thinking. Sex and violence were the accepted norm for the ones who held the power. Control of others was their expression of this power.

As empires began to spread into new lands never before contemplated, a new breed of man was discovered. These were the so-called savages. These people were unlike the civilized people. These people were called savages because they didn't make "proper" use of the land and its inherent wealth. Rather, they chose to live in harmony with the world as it were.

It was also noted that these people had darker skin than the civilized man. Surely, this was a result of their sinful souls, many believed. They were considered ignorant to the generally accepted belief that man was above his environment and were thus judged as the rest of the animal kingdom, a resource to be used, exploited.

Their likeness to civilized man led many to believe they were only lost souls and had to be converted to God-fearing men. The advent of the missionary sprung upon us. The savages were enslaved to build the churches they were to worship in. And they were maimed and tortured until they either died or converted to the religion of these invaders of their land, their saviors.

These savages knew how to fight, and they mostly did so in a defensive manner. But their primitive weapons were of no match to those of the technologically advanced intruders. Over the course of the next few hundred years, they were all but wiped out. Their spirit or the spirit of their cultures had been broken. Their souls had been won over, but the color of their skin remained to remind the white man they were not to be trusted. Discrimination of race had set in.

When man was in but small groups, he received the first signs of error in the form of the priests. He failed to recognize the signs. Later came the messiahs or messengers. Again, he had failed to retain the message; and he grew in his error to create the great empires. The third wave of signs came with the discovery of these savages in their innocence of living in harmony with their world. For the third time, mankind failed to see the error.

With no more new lands to be conquered, the advent of the empire began to die away. For the first time, humanity was seeing the limits of this world. The concept of nations was taking hold to replace the empires. And for the first time, man began to look to other worlds as a real possibility; although the technology to do so would not be coming any time soon.

It was during this time that war would reach around the planet, and the need was seen to create an alliance between independent nations. The strength of these alliances was hampered by the greed of nations still. They showed themselves to be imperfect in a world that refused to feel satisfied. The end of free expansionism also caused the people of these predatory nations to focus on the individual more than ever.

This self-reflection by the common people brought about movements toward establishing the equality of mankind, meaning all of mankind. This was the first step toward humanism. These movements met with great resistance from the establishment. More so was the resistance in the beginning. With time, however, the acceptance spread. And most agreed that these ideals held something legitimate and necessary; although, in practice there remained a lot of failure to carry out the intention.

There came the day when space was finally reached. We had broken free from the bounds of this world. It was the intention of war and control, again, which had fueled this intent. It was the conquest of space that would finally bring nations together like never before. It was found to be too costly for any single nation and yet too valuable to let go. An uneasy peace grew between the strong predator nations.

Still the violence grew, but in a new form now. It would be the weaker nations that would begin to rebel against their lot in this new global village. Inequity was now the subject that fueled their anger. They refused to be pawns of the predator nations. They refused to be used as resources, to be raped by foreign greed. Their technology was not up to par with that of the predator nations and their allies. They were no match in a conventional kind of war. In their desperation, they turned to terrorism to deliver fear into the hearts of the people of these other nations.

This began happening at a time when many of the common people of these predator nations were already growing weary of their own governments' motivations. The governments of these strong nations were becoming true bureaucracies, entities unto themselves, which held little accountability to the common man's ideals.

JEFFREY B. BRANDT

Many of these common people began to practice self-reflection in the wake of their disillusionment with their governments. Much of this self-reflection, however, was misguided and was cause for many to then exercise victimism or playing into self-pity support groups. These groups consisted of others who felt the same as they. This only carried the nations further into decadence as it put trust of others into a tailspin; this set the stage for predatory lawsuits of every kind within the same culture. This only increased the feeling of hopelessness in the masses.

Many in the Western cultures turned to inquire about the Eastern religions that tended to place their focus inward toward the soul. This was becoming increasingly viable due to the capability of worldwide communication. Being almost entirely unfamiliar with the details of these religions, Western people tended to dabble in the most superficial aspects of several of them at any time, primarily Taoism, Hinduism, and Buddhism. As well, they now got a new perspective of Christianity, with the focus on the historical Christ. This led to a new movement in spiritualism. The focus was on the messengers' words and tended to overlook the rituals of the established religions.

It was the self that was now in the spotlight, in an external world that was becoming increasingly hostile and growing more so, exponentially, by the day. It was in these times that mankind began to make a concerted effort to find his way home in a spiritual sense. Perhaps this was forced upon him by the magnitude of the emptiness he was experiencing from his external world. This journey would prove to be a difficult one as he had wandered so far and had created a world of illusions within illusions.

This was becoming a world not of individuals but of unreal entities. The power of governments and laws were becoming more relevant than the individuals they were meant to serve. It was humanmade insanity on a massive and growing scale. Our creation had emancipated itself as it took on its own life force.

With the depth of so many levels of sincerity and confusion, it was only natural, human, to see the rise of many false religions or philosophies in these times. Humanity was at the threshold of evolving into something new. The strength of the global powers continued to grow, led by the predator nations and fought by the lesser nations and their terrorism, while new "secret" societies began to develop within these macrocultures.

The inspiration of these new secret societies lay in the idea of creating a new breed of man. This new breed, the originators hoped, would achieve the qualities of the great messiahs of the past. He would be an enlightened soul, able to create a better world for himself and others.

Some would attempt to accomplish this, however, through some external means, which in essence is no different than what they were struggling against to begin with. Selective breeding, for many generations, was hoped to eventually lead to the possibility of creating a manmade messiah or even a human god.

Still, it was the fear of giving in to something greater than ourselves that was the cause for many abominations to be created during these times. In essence, nothing had changed. In detail, humanity came to know the most fearsome plots in its history. These new breeds would eventually bear fruit to some of the most power-hungry leaders ever known and set about a struggle to survive against humanity itself. There would be no place to hide. This would become the revelation, the apocalypse.

This is the world as I see it, and I see no deviance from it or what lies ahead. The era of terrorism has solidified with the unprecedented and successful attack on the world's strongest nation. It will remain with us now, and it will only become stronger.

We are at the point today when we may begin seeing signs of germination of these false religions or philosophies, if we remain alert.

These will be based on the ideas of desperate and disillusioned souls, and they will grow strong. And the secret societies will play only a subtle part of our existence for many generations to come before they will manifest into something greater than the unenlightened establishment can control. This will bring a new kind of terror, which few people today have yet contemplated. This is the destiny of humanity.

Destiny, I see as something unchangeable for humanity as a whole. Many have expressed an idea of a divine intervention that will end our worldly struggle. I see no divine intervention in our future. Not in this sense. Those who do, I believe, have a mistaken outlook on what exactly divinity is. There is nothing relevant to divinity within the context of the physical. It is something subtler than this. We are directing our future within this context of the physical. Only we are responsible for what we are experiencing or that which we will experience within this realm.

Anything we may do here will have no effect on the divine, including that part of ourselves which is divine. The divine is untouchable from a physical standpoint. If we could only understand this, all of our fears would lose their power over us. And we could live in peace as was the original intention. Forget about the world. Begin to see your true existence within this realm and the beauty which lies within all things.

It is not in the rest of humanity where we need to place our focus. So long as we continue to focus on the rest of humanity, we have not changed in essence. We continue in the error of original sin, the urge to take control. This, I believe, is where we need to have faith in greater things. This does not mean that we are not to work for a better world, on the contrary. What I am saying is that the path to that which we seek is not always in the direction we would likely believe it to be. Remember we have created a world of illusions within illusions.

Paradox

How much pain is created in people when they fail to realize that the only change they will ever make is within themselves? We base our lives around trying to make things better "out there," and we find nothing but isolation. We look to ourselves. Let everything out there go, and we find continuity. Does this sound like a paradox? Maybe it is so, but there is a lot of truth to be had in this line of thought.

It is only when we realize the weight of what so many messiahs have said before about letting go of what is out there to place our focus upon what is within our own hearts that we will see the essence within ourselves. When we see our original sin, we may work on that. Only in this way may we truly change anything in essence.

The church is the strongest force of humanity, but it is a force of pure illusion. It is a manmade institution. Remember this. No messiah has condoned these institutions, and many have warned us about them. Their motives are not, in essence, any different than that which they so condemn. Hypocrisy is rampant. It uses the shield of ignorance to propagate none other than itself. Nothing has done more to pervert the message of the messenger than the religion created around that messenger and his message.

The church is full of symbolism and ritual, which can only be of this world. This world is one of illusion. We must walk away from the illusion, away from the church, and closer to truth, closer to God. We do so through our example and only through our example. There is pain to be had on this journey, but the pain does not come from nearing the destination that which we seek. It comes from leaving behind the source that which we perceive ourselves to be.

We have grown comfortable in our illusion, and leaving it behind signifies sacrifice. It means taking personal responsibility for our part in propagating this illusion. We are like children who want to break free and be independent while the price of that independence seems to be painful. It is about responsibility. It is a path no other may walk for us. Think of our current situation as an addiction.

We are addicted to our illusions. They have brought us justification for our problems and so many wars, and they have ensured the continuance of our destructive ways. They have been the cause for us to feel isolated and violated by all that exists around us. Because of our illusions, we feel only separation from our world.

Be not content with what you see around you. See it as a sign of how beautiful letting go can be. You are in this world, but you are not of this world. Stop living in fear as if this is the world to which you pertain. Choose your path and walk it proudly that others may see your example. Be content with yourself. Be true to yourself and know that everything out there will be taken care of. Whatever may happen in this world is a part of this world. It is in the plan of this world, not your plan. Whatever you might do to try to change the world will do nothing for you or the world. You will only be propagating that which you so disdain.

The best you can do for yourself or the world is one and the same; observe the world around you, look into yourself to find those aspects of the world you sense are wrong, and change them within yourself. Then you let the world go on with faith. Share yourself freely with any neighbor in need. Accept each soul as you would have them accept you, and work only on your example.

You hold the key to paradise, but it is your paradise to which you hold the key. Every living soul has their own key, and only their key will open the door for them. Show them this through your example.

To see the truth, you must focus not on the details seen with the mind but on the essence seen with the heart. In essence lies the key to divine truth. Divine truth is the only truth. It is the truth we see not in the actions of others but in their manner. If you cannot see their manner, you cannot see the truth behind their actions. In this way, no action can be cause to judge another soul.

The most divine of souls may be troubled into committing or at least considering an irreverent act. This act or consideration, a bad soul does not make. Concern yourself not with judgment of another soul. Your purpose is to learn from the essence of what you see. Focus on yourself, nothing more. You are the example of what you believe and whether you choose to propagate that which you judge or to show a better way. The choice is, was, and always will be yours and only yours.

Commune for the purpose of clarifying your vision and strengthening your convictions. But do not lose sight of the fact that you are ultimately responsible for your own destiny, and each soul is ultimately responsible for his. Share and accept.

My message is to the hearts of people, not directed to any government or church. It is only to the people, and it is only to those who will see it. The message is one of acceptance. This is to say letting go of the need to control. The answer to what we seek cannot be found in a church. Nor can it be found in any government. Only within the individual soul may we truly find the answer we seek. Only through living for ourselves will we be able to help any other.

This is not anarchy. Those who may say that it is only express ignorance derived from the fear of losing control. This fear is based on not understanding the first truth. This is the truth of history. Nothing I have said here conflicts in any way with what has been said by the great messiahs. Any who may doubt this would do well to look into the words of those messiahs; but do so directly, not through the corresponding religions, as here you will likely find conflict. I remind you: Religion is an institution created by mankind, and many messiahs have addressed this issue with equal warning.

I would also like to remind you that when I say to practice acceptance, this means without exception. Acceptance of church and government included, as they are as much a part of this world as humanity itself. Your responsibility is toward yourself, and it ends with sharing your ideals with others through your example. You can deny your reverence to these institutions without condemning the souls behind them or refusing to pay what they require of you in a worldly form.

Paying taxes, for example, does not compromise who you are or where you are going. If you are required to give something that is not of you but of this world, do so. Just remember, it is their game; and you are in it. You are giving them something they had created in the first place. This need be of no concern to you. You are giving nothing of yourself in returning what is not of you. You may allow whatever that does not compromise your responsibility toward yourself.

If you are required to do or give something that would compromise yourself or your beliefs, refuse, but do so in a passive way; although this may very well result in being incarcerated or even executed. An example that comes to mind is the requirement to serve in the military during wartime. We are to serve for the purpose of killing or destroying lives. For what purpose? We are not serving ourselves here. Neither are we serving another soul. We are serving an illusion.

Who am I to justify taking the life of someone I have never even met and know nothing about? For all I know, under any other circumstances, this soul may have turned out to be my best friend. I don't feel justified in judging each soul I may find on a battlefield. And judge them by what criteria? Maybe by the clothing they are wearing or by the color of their skin? Let's get real here please. I have had good friends from many different places and many different colors of skin and kinds of clothing. Are they trying to kill me as well? What more could one expect in the arena of a battlefield? They are serving the same illusion as I am in that moment. I am a part of that life, which I am trying to kill.

The accepted mentality of defending our freedom or way of life means nothing in essence here. Kill this man because of something his people did to my people? What kind of isolationist logic is this? I know for a fact that I don't want someone judging me for acts committed by what they consider to be "my people." I'm not at all pleased with the way many other Americans, Mexicans, or white people, or even men, have acted. And I am an American, a Mexican, and white. And I am a man.

In deciding you will not do something that would compromise yourself or your beliefs, such as the above example, I remind you to do so in a passive way. Always remember, it is only through your example that you express your true beliefs.

> If I am against anything at all, it would be that I am against demonstrating what one is against. A simple opinion would suffice, and, even then, only when solicited. I think what we really need to do is start demonstrating what we are for.

Chapter IV

Religion

Arguments about the validity of religion have been around for about as long as religion itself, I would imagine. I find these arguments to be rather lame at best. Religion is not something to be debated. There is likely nothing more personal than religion for those who practice it. Likely as well, it is for those who don't. It is a topic loaded with personal fire. Few are those who really don't have anything to say for either case. And fewer still may be those who are convinced to change their religious views by argument.

The concept of religion really is not as conflictive as the rituals surrounding the concept have made it out to be. These rituals then are truly the basis of the arguments. Anyone who thinks otherwise really doesn't understand what he is arguing for. In essence, religion doesn't need to be in conflict with anything that we may wish for ourselves or for others. This would include even our most material thoughts: business, relationships, carnal pleasure, etc. It is in the moment when we begin to impose the rites of religion that conflict manifests itself. It is in what we create around the essence where our concept of religion begins to fail us.

The basic message of any messenger has always been clear. Live your life true to the laws that govern the natural. Until you can do this, your focus should always be on yourself. Share yourself, but do not impose. Trust completely in the fact that the natural will continue in spite of what we may be looking for. It is only when we realize this completely that we will be in harmony with our world or any world.

It doesn't matter if the religion we are concerned with is Hinduism, Taoism, Buddhism, Christianity, Islam, Judaism or any of the other major religions. It all comes down to personal decisions based on respect for ourselves and for what is around us.

Religion can mean many different things. Almost as many concepts exist as there are cultures, if not individuals. Religion is usually the belief in a higher force and the ability to communicate with this force. This may be anything from ancestors to a god or many gods, or even to some entity within our physical world.

In essence, it really doesn't matter what or even if you worship. The concept of worship is, after all, only a rite built around the essence of religion. The idea of having reverence in itself, even if it is only for yourself, is sufficient to be labeled religion for the purposes of this book. The message of this section is simple and to the point; in being true to any religion, in its essence, there is no sense in forcing or imposing your beliefs on anyone. If you choose to claim a religion, remember it is your choice. Don't make the error of forcing your choice upon others. In doing thus, it will not be their choice; and you will only have tainted your expression of what you believed to be the truth.

The truth is not yours or mine. The truth simply is. And another person's choice to see or not to see this truth will always be his or her choice. The world can and does give signs as to what is truth. When we live in true harmony with the world, we become just another of these signs. The more perfect our harmony, the more perfect we become as a sign or expression of this truth. If we truly give reverence to that which is, we can see there is no better expression of our belief than living it as it is. And the moment we impose force to this expression, we distort it.

It is sad to live in truth when we are immersed in a world of illusion. It feels so human, the desire to intervene. Understand it is this desire to intervene, which is very strong, that is the part of us that has created this world of illusion in the first place. It is that same part in others that manifests in what we see as ill-guided attempts to save the world at best or as downright evil at its worst. Accept this desire for it is a part of being human, but realize it is the part that separates us from the perfection of our world that will simply continue in spite of what we do. The lesson has always been there. It is up to us to see this lesson.

In taking this lesson in, we find consolation in even the most difficult situations we may face. This may include even a separation or a divorce or the death of a loved one. The isolation we once sensed begins to dissipate. It is replaced by a sense of unity with our world that transcends whatever separation we may be experiencing. This is because we begin to see the world as a continuum, not as a series of isolated events that change our outlook with every happening. We begin to see the world for what it is, a loving entity with only our well-being in mind.

With this outlook, our journey becomes one of tranquility. We seem to know that everything has its purpose, and there really is no evil out there waiting for us to let our guard down so it can pounce. Life becomes our friend and confidant, our companion. Coming to understand this lesson is like coming home in a spiritual sense. Understanding this lesson is the key to understanding the third truth. The third truth is religion. We understand that nothing needs to be judged. We only need to experience and grow within this experience.

BELIEVE

Someday I'll cry. But until then, I'll keep living the same. I reach for the sky. Life on earth can be too insane. We don't love each other. We don't even try. We put off all our dreams until the day we die. In a word, we call it faith, but a word is all that it is. What's mine is mine. What's yours is yours. And what's hers will never be his.

Our only friend is death. And death we truly fear. It's one thing we can count on. In our own way, we hold it dear. We know life. And we know it well, but what comes after that? Who has lived to tell? Is it just a mystery? Or did he really see? Who am I to say he lied? Could he really be? The questions are there, but do we care? We either do or don't believe.

Chapter V

THE MESSIAH'S LIFE

Can one really choose to live the life of a messiah? What exactly is a messiah? A messiah is, by definition, a messenger of divine truth, a liberator. Historically, these messengers have delivered their messages primarily through the example of their lives. In this sense, yes, we can live the life of a messiah. But the messiah usually suffers a great deal on behalf of humanity. Given that one is likely going to suffer on behalf of humanity, why would one choose to live the life of a messiah? Because along with this suffering comes a sense of security that cannot be taken away. This is something we all seek at some level within our psyche, although we may not even be aware of it. If we are not aware of it, this could be a sign that we are not ready for it.

It is in our nature to live this reality. It is a part of us. And when we are able to live this reality, we see that any suffering we do experience is not real but a part of the illusion in which we as a part of humanity have created. The suffering is all around us, but it is not within us. This can only be a subjective experience; then again, everything we experience is just that, a subjective experience. Life is full of suffering. The more we try to avoid this suffering, the more it seems we will eventually experience

JEFFREY B. BRANDT

it. Allow it to pass over you, by you, and through you. When it runs its course, you will find that only beauty remains. This beauty is the truth of what always exists.

Life is beautiful. Even in the crumbling of two giant towers in which thousands of people die or in the exploding space shuttle with its crew onboard, we can witness a certain beauty. How many have not seen the beauty in the explosion of an atomic bomb with its impressive mushroom cloud? This beauty can be seen by anyone who chooses to see it with an unattached eye. The beauty is there as well as the sadness in knowing the motivation behind the creation of such an incident. It is the same with every incident. One can find within each experience the full spectrum of interpretation. The birth of a child can be seen as a horrifying experience if one would look at it from the child's perspective. The birth of a child tends to bring happiness to all while the child cries. The death of someone in the family tends to manifest sorrow in those who are left behind while the deceased lies in peace.

The best thing about living the life of a messiah is the clear perception it brings of our present situation. There is no confusion. There is no hesitancy to accept the present situation as it is and to go from there. This same gift, however, can be the most difficult aspect of living the life of a messiah. It is this gift that often causes the messiah to live a life parallel to the ways of the world without actually living as a part of the world.

His purpose is to live, experience, and share himself. This can be most challenging when he desires the intimate, physical company of another human being. This is a difficult thing to find without compromise. This is especially so in our Western culture.

It is difficult, yes, but it is not impossible. Because it is so difficult, I believe, many have promoted the idea of celibacy. The ideals behind this act appear to have been greatly distorted by various churches in their believing it is something absolutely necessary for all priests, monks, and nuns. The act of celibacy, I see, is a personal choice, as is any choice we may make. The choice of pro or con concerning celibacy can be equally honorable.

In either case, the life of a messiah can be a lonely life. Not because one feels he has separated himself from the rest of humanity, rather, because he feels the rest of humanity has separated itself from him. The resulting feeling is nearly the same. The enlightened one can relate to all people the same. He understands them. This is a quality that attracts people. They feel drawn by his wisdom, his confidence, and his simplicity.

At the same time, however, people cannot seem to relate to him. They cannot grasp his sometimes unorthodox way of confronting life's situations. This is especially true when it means he will come out of a situation being condemned or even hurt by its corruptness. They cannot understand his unconditional acceptance of the way things are while he continues on his way, as if innocently oblivious to what is truly happening. This quickly becomes too much for most to deal with.

> He is dedicated to working for a better world but only in passive form. He never forces his way upon others or condemns them. His actions and words are one and the same. Though he may say very little in the way of words, his message tends to impact others in a most profound way.

In living the life of a messiah, temptation does not cease. The awareness of this temptation becomes heightened, but we continue to see the choice. Beyond having greater awareness of temptation, we also see the consequences of ceding to that temptation, perhaps, more clearly than the average mortal being. This is a game that will not cease while we exist on this plane, and it is a game that we may tire of playing.

The purer one's life becomes, the closer one feels to death. The difference between life and death tends to lose any great significance for us as we understand that our position in this life is far less trivial and more personal than those around us see it. We may often see death more as an eventual relief from the trivialities we must face on a daily basis. This is because we are still a part of humanity, which in its largest part tends not to think of life as anything other than work and recreation. This can be cause for a great deal of frustration as we begin to feel limited in our opportunity to express ourselves while having to continue facing those mundane tasks a "normal" life requires.

Making a living can become one of the most frustrating experiences for a sincere soul who has something to share and the drive to share it. Making a living usually requires a good portion of our time. This requirement can cause us to feel as a slave to time. Keep in mind that even this frustrating experience has its purpose. It shows us we still have something more to learn before we can consider ourselves truly enlightened.

A truly enlightened person is a master of dealing with reality. He deals not in illusion but only in what is real. At the same time, he understands the illusion that is all around him. He accepts it as a part of the way of this world while he knows it is not his world. He may always strive to improve his position in this world, although he is at peace with his lot in it. He accepts where he is presently and always goes from there. If he needs to decide between compromising his material position or his ideals, there is no hesitation on his part. He will let the opportunity go by without remorse, and he will stand forever by his ideals. This is the part of the enlightened person that the average person understands least.

A truly enlightened person must understand just how uncommon his way is, and he must understand what this means to the average human being. Meeting a truly enlightened person can be a frustrating, even frightening experience for most. To the enlightened person, truth may seem to be the simplest and most obvious thing to see, and calmly reacting to the truth may be a completely natural experience. This is not always the case. At least, it may not be for the common soul. Even the most well-intentioned souls may have great difficulties in facing the truth within themselves. It is of vital importance to the truly enlightened person to understand themselves from the perspective of those who may not be so enlightened. This can be the most challenging goal in the enlightened one's journey of life.

If you consider yourself to be an enlightened soul, you may have noticed a certain pattern that tends to repeat itself with mostly everyone you meet. They come. They become intrigued by your ways. The endless list of questions about your perspective on life begins. Their self-doubt begins to surge within them. The condemnation and abandonment follow. And you are alone again. What goes on in the minds of most when meeting and getting to know this uncommon person? This can be the million-dollar question.

For the common person, we have a difficult time understanding that different perspectives of reality exist. Our world is full of conflict for this reason more so than any other. We tend to relate with only those people who share our views of the world, and we judge the rest as being blind to reality as it truly is. We place many conditions on reality. We reinforce these conditions with our own experiences as well as those of people we know or even on hearsay when it fits our needs. Experience is our tool for interpreting our world. We see with the mind and ignore what the heart tells us. This is especially so in the Western cultures, which tend to be more materialistic and external in their vision of what they consider to be reality.

When meeting someone who doesn't rely on the external world, we feel we have met an alien of sorts. This person is like no other you have met before. He shows no fear and never seems to anger or express apathy, as if these qualities had completely vanished from his person. He may appear to be as normal as any other person on a superficial level. It is when you begin getting to know this person that the truth subtly yet profoundly makes itself known.

As this truth becomes known, you may begin to feel somewhat uncomfortable. This is because the realness of this person can be, shall we say, overwhelming. There is something rather intimidating for most in meeting someone who is so real. We begin to play possibilities through our mind: "What could be the motivating factor behind this obsessive charade of being so good, of being so much better than the rest?" Did he say he was better than the rest? "Well, no but . . ."

This person does not allow himself to be seduced by trivialities that might interfere with how he interprets what he knows to be correct. The reaction of those around him will not distract him in the least. He seems to have no need for approval from the outside world. This, at first, may draw one in close to this person as it expresses his personal strength. After time, however, this very same aspect of him may tend to diminish any desire to be near this person as one's own feelings of inadequacy or impurity begin to make themselves known.

This is when most normal people decide to leave the strange one behind. Their reasoning is that they feel too insecure about their own future with this person who would just as soon let the world screw them over than take advantage of a situation now and then, especially if it means possibly screwing someone else over in the process. After all, this sort of thing happens all the time. Why does he (or she) insist on being so different in this respect?

This is the end of the cycle. It is a cycle that those strange ones know only too well. Their lives are lonely, but there is no other way for them to be. Compromise is not an option. They are in this world, but they are not of this world. It is only the things of this world they are losing out on.

In essence, they know only they can screw themselves over; and this is something they will never do. Yes, they feel the loss. But they don't feel it the same as the average person. They feel the loss for the world. They feel the pain of the world but not for themselves. This is because they are the ones who truly live for the world. They choose to suffer on behalf of the world because they know what they receive is well worth this price. They have achieved a stability of self that cannot be dissuaded. And they know this is something we all seek on some level of our psyche. And like the world itself, they continue on, only waiting for the opportunity to shine in the heart of another human being.

THE SEED

My body rips as my mind soars, like the tearing of the shell from the seed within. I am losing my grip on the world around me as it crumbles into infinity in a fashion that seems beyond even my control. And, as the same, I must continue to strive for what I have always known. As this becomes even more real to me, I see even more obviously how oblivious this world is to it; and I ask, "Why must this be?" Truly, man has sinned, but why am I to see and I alone?

God is so gracious. I can only hope to be so as he. It is through his grace that I shall find the strength to be so gracious. For it is he that has experienced all that I have and yet remains so.

To be his only begotten son is beyond any blessing imaginable, and to see in any other way is impossible. And though the heart cannot sin, it is the body, born of and into this evil world, which is torn with the constant struggle between the forces of the divine and the forces of the worldly. The body knows the divine will prevail; but, being of evil fiber, it instinctively seeks carnal satisfaction.

The forces of instinct are great, but they are temporary. We are free to choose our own path in life, whether it be in the name of God, our father, or otherwise.

God is our creator, and all is possible in him. It is by his grace that we were created in his image, and his creation is perfect. It is by our sin that we have lost faith in him, and we have put faith in our own creation above his. And our creation is imperfect. His creation is eternal and self-healing while ours is temporary and self-destructive. His creation is true and of himself while ours is false and borrowed.

Being created in his image, we have the potential to create of ourselves. By choosing to attach ourselves to our sins, we continue to be sinners. We create in conflict with his creation. Only a creation which is in harmony with that which we are of in every respect is true and everlasting.

Chapter VI

CHILDREN ARE THE TEACHERS

I would like to begin this journey by inviting you to return to your childhood. There is magic in youth. From the child's perspective, there is mystery and adventure to be found in performing every task, save having to take out the trash. Come to think of it, even this task can become an adventure. It can become a show of strength or a chance to exhibit our braveness in daring to go outside into the darkness of the night. Or it can become a journey to a faraway place. Can you remember this? If the answer is yes, I congratulate you on not leaving your childhood memories too far behind; and I smile to myself because it means my job of helping you to recall that innate wisdom we each have within us will be easier.

Every child comes into this world with a spark, an intense and insatiable desire to experience his world in its every aspect. He wants to see it and taste it. He wants to feel and hear every detail, not just once but again and again. His world is as alive as he is. Everything is full of life. When a child wakes up in the morning, he is ready to begin his day full of energy. He doesn't want to walk. He would rather run. When he lies down to sleep, he sleeps immediately. There exists nothing to interrupt his flow of living until we begin to teach him what he "needs" to learn.

Every child is open to any stimulation. This is the primordial essence of his or her innocence. This same essence continues to exist within each one of us, no matter how dormant it may appear to be. Here, there exists no fear, anger, apathy, or hate. There is only the purest expression of life, of love.

A child will accept any fate with equal response. This means any culture, religion, economic status, or social class in which he or she is raised will be considered the norm of his or her world. Our performance as parents, family, community, nation, race, gender, social class, etc. has been not to expand on this, or even to freely allow it, but to limit every aspect of this expression. We have instilled our morals, our beliefs, our prejudices, and our fears in our children since we ourselves had received them from our parents, family, community, nation, race, gender, social class, etc. It is this condition that breeds our separatist view of our world.

It is in our attempt to bring order to all of these classifications where we create what we have termed *problems*. The still-innocent child doesn't see these problems in the world until we show him. More than this, when the child does begin to see these problems, he sees only their essence. His mind is not tainted by the details we have experienced and by which we use to judge these problems and the world. We look at a problem, and we see a history that only becomes more complicated. We don't seem to realize that every other individual has his own history to inject.

The child only sees the problem itself. For this reason, his solutions are simple and direct. His solutions don't entail all of the conditions that only serve to ensure future confrontations of the same problem which we, as adults, so often come up with. Ask a child how to make a safer world, and he will tell you, "Stop fighting."

The more we exert control upon our world, the more we end up being controlled by the world. This really is all we have to learn. But, more than learn it, we must accept it and live it. Until we do, we will never be free by any definition. This is a paradox which we find unfathomable as adults. It is a truth which cannot be understood by the "mature" and logical mind.

This is where we may look to the mind of the child. The child's mind is not logical until we make it so. The still-innocent child has no notion of the prejudiced mind. He accepts a person of any color or characteristic. He doesn't see problems as we do. He only sees new experiences and is only too eager to experience them.

There are dangers in our world, and these dangers are very real. Letting a child jump into any situation could be even fatal. Clearly, we cannot just allow a child to do as the child would please without considering the consequences of the action. But we need to be aware of what it is we are trying to accomplish in telling a child no. Can we guide without compromising the integrity of a child's global-oriented insight, without limiting the essential manner in which he views the world, without being detrimental to his puritan innocence?

It helps to understand why a child does what he or she does or even why any one of us do what we do. People generally tend to follow certain patterns of behavior throughout their lives. These patterns could be described as life stages. Understanding them and how each one can build upon the following stages can be very enlightening. The following description is not based on any scientific thing. It is based solely on my personal observations but may be of use just the same.

Life stages:

From the first few days up to a week or two, a baby pretty much sleeps most of the time, only waking long enough to eat before continuing to sleep. As a baby sleeps, their mind is working a great deal, assimilating information sent to it by way of the senses of hearing, smell, taste, and touch. The sense of hearing would be the most influential at this time.

Volume of stimulation is very important at this stage to set the pattern for the baby's expression of self. Will the child be loud and boisterous, or will it be quiet and docile? Will this child be consistent in his or her character?

This pattern actually begins during the pregnancy while the baby is still inside the mother's womb. What kind of music does the mother listen to, if any? What kind of environment does she live in? Stress level plays an important role here in the child's ability to adapt to situations and to interpret his outside world.

A few days to a week or two after birth, the baby will begin to leave this incessant sleep period behind and will become more in tune with his or her world. The eyes become a more important source of information than ever before as the baby begins to focus on and observe his surroundings. Soon he will begin reaching for objects to feel them for their texture and size. The next step is to try to put these objects into the mouth. At first, the mouth is used more as an extended form of touching things; but soon the baby will discover that the world of taste enters through the mouth. A young child's primary motivation for learning is pleasure. Is it any wonder we associate taste with pleasure?

This period of exploration continues through the period of learning to crawl and later to walk as the motor skills are better developed. With the ability to walk, the toddler begins to feel independence for the first time. With this, he will begin to enter into the stage of copying others. This is a period of kinesthetic learning and of fantasy for the child, and it is also the best time to develop the imagination and begin working with intuition. Decent role models are absolutely essential here. Things like temper and social ability are pretty much set during this period.

This copying period lasts well into childhood and is the period when many social problems develop in the child's character. It is important to realize that the majority of these actions, which we consider problems, actually developed as a result of the critical first steps in their development. The loud obnoxious child, the misfit, the crybaby, etc. are the result of a hectic beginning filled with stress and a lack of structure in the daily routine, even before the child learned to crawl. A daily pattern is so vital to assuring a well-adjusted development of the child's character. Besides this, we must consider what he is doing.

His actions are becoming more of how he interprets the actions of others around him in his life. He is experimenting with different roles to find recognition as an individual. It is not the child whom we need to address at this point. It is only his interpretation of things as well as the role we have played that which inspired this development of his behavior. Aspects such as temper and control, domination and intimidation, carelessness and respect are manifestations of the seeds we have planted through our own example for the child to follow.

As the child begins to go out into the world independently, he will begin to feel the awkwardness to a varying degree. How much depends upon the development of his character in the first few years of his life. Negative experiences early on will only cause this period to be experienced more intensely as well as prolong the duration. A well-adjusted child will barely experience this stage. In our modern, Western culture, this period has become an extended stage due to the lack of foundation in the early years of a child's life. Social awkwardness has become the norm for many.

Competition can be a two-sided coin. In our culture, we seem to have extracted only the most evil of these two sides. Our focus has been primarily on winning for ourselves without much acknowledgment for the other. We consider in competition where there is a winner, there must be a loser. This has also been where our own hypocrisy has been most noted. And, believe me, it is noted by the child. Even the most poorly adjusted child sees this hypocrisy, and he learns to react accordingly. This has been cause for a violent society, more so than any other single factor. We are not out for each other's well-being as much as we would like to believe we are. This is from the fear that we each experience, which in turn comes from our own lack of adjustment in our early childhood years.

This competitive situation can last a lifetime for some. Usually this is most noted in our careers or criminal records. It is a part of us, and we tend to identify with it the most. Though the tendency is we least understand this aspect of ourselves. This is our ego. Even many of those who seem to be fighting for a noble cause are really no further along than so many career criminals. It is the ego that they serve in essence.

A very common example of this is the great number of nonprofit or charity organizations that exist, where the founders live very comfortable lives at the expense of the money given by the people who support those causes. Some of these salaries are truly appalling. And they may be even more so when we consider the many extras the founders receive for serving their cause. Are they really serving their cause, or is their cause, in reality, serving them?

For those who make it beyond the competitive stage, we see a calm that seems to be increasingly rare in our world. It is a calm that is derived from being content with one's lot in life. It has no relevance to the outside world. This calm can only come from within. It is a sad fact that most will not reach this stage without first experiencing at least a few rather large setbacks in life. These setbacks seem to be necessary. It causes us to refocus our attention on what is really important in our lives.

Feeling secure with one's life doesn't need to mean the end of the road. In fact one of the greatest joys of life can be the searching for something more. This can be especially so when one is not pressured by thoughts of survival.

This is the point where nearly all of us should be today with the current technology we have to ensure our survival against the natural dangers that exist. Even the man in the street really has little to fear in the way of weather, animals, or starvation. This is one of the saddest realizations one can make concerning the path humanity has chosen or, more specifically, what man has chosen to do with his position in this world. We have created such an array of artificial threats that keep us from enjoying this most inspiring stage of life.

Finally, we come to the stage of self. This is the stage of enlightenment. The few that have reached this stage no longer live as the rest live. They are the teachers. Their students are all those who know them. They have much to teach, though they don't always teach in the traditional manner. It is their example from which we may learn. Their example is one that knows no international or cultural borders. They are truly human in the most natural sense. They speak to us all. They speak to the heart. Their language is one. It is one of love, of giving, and of acceptance.

Children naturally live this stage until they begin to copy others. What they have to copy is not perfect; and when they begin to copy, they begin to be less than perfect. This is cause for the stages of awkwardness and later, competition. These stages are not necessary, and they are not inherent to our nature. They are periods of self-questioning and insecurities. It is in our failure to see this that we affect the lives of our children in the most negative way. We propagate a future replete with insecurities and difficulties. We need to realize just where we are in relation to what truly is to avoid this. Our world is not evil. We are who we are regardless of what the world may be.

Simply shun that which is not pleasant to you as the child within would do. Live your own life and share yourself incessantly. Don't allow the

JEFFREY B. BRANDT

world to be your excuse to change accordingly. Remember that child in you knows the truth. Trying to deny this truth will only bring difficulties later in your life. Sigmund Freud based his lifework around this concept of manifestations of undischarged emotional energy associated with forgotten psychic traumas.

Live every moment for what it's worth. Reach out to it, feel it, taste it, and devour it every waking moment. Accept your emotions without reservation. Keep the spark alive, and you will do well in life. Follow your dreams, and make them happen. Don't concern yourself with the realities of others. This is your fantasy.

A child can express anger and happiness with the same intensity within seconds of the other. Whatever they are experiencing, they are experiencing with every fiber in that moment. Whatever they are experiencing, they really are experiencing it. They are always real, even more so than we; although we reject their fantasies as something less than real. We choose our sorrowful fantasies over theirs and teach them to do the same. We have reversed the roles, and we refuse to give up control to the truly wise ones. We have rebelled against the way we were meant to be.

Don't be so quick to give up that child inside. That child is your best ally in a world gone awry. Stay close and stay tight. Love yourself without questions that will surely be posed by those less secure individuals around you. You know your dreams, and you have the confidence to make them come true. All you really need is time to understand what we have done to this world. But answers to this mess, you don't need. You already possess them. Believe in yourself, and follow your own heart. No other can give you your own key.

These are not wise words that have come from an old sage who has lived his life. Rather, they are wise words carried over from an unforgotten youth, which holds inherent and universal wisdom. This wisdom is timeless, as we are in essence.

It takes a stubborn child to hold these truths against an ignorant world. Let us learn from this. And let us make this world less ignorant and more welcoming to those young lives that have come to visit us. Let us never forget that the child is the teacher.

Let us give this world to the children, and stop trying to keep it for ourselves. We are the ones who know not how to appreciate this gift. It is a gift that flows, and we are but that which tries to do no more than stop this flow. We will never succeed until we allow it to carry us home. Home. What a sweet sound.

LIFE

Life is a gamble we all have to take. The only way to escape is to meet our ultimate fate. When we come into this world, we are bound by no law. How we limit ourselves becomes our own personal flaw. If we grant ourselves the chance to feel true love from within, it can make our lives worth living.

We have all we need, an innate part of our being. As the eyes of our soul, the heart is for seeing. We blind ourselves not by passion of the moment but from restraint of emotion tied to fashion of the times. Free yourself now, and keep this priceless treasure. Go with your heart that pays no heed to measure. Love one another as you would love only yourself. Give all you can from within and without. Life is no mystery, as we only can see by living with love in perfect harmony. Life is no gamble for those who know. The answers are there only waiting to show.

Chapter VII

PROPHECY

There is a power in prophecy that we must recognize. This power is not to be taken lightly. Prophecy in its purest sense is not creative; however, it becomes creative the moment we try to own it. It becomes a tool, which has been used ignorantly by the masses. And it propagates further ignorance in those who do not understand the power inherent to the mind.

This is because prophecy tends to be self-fulfilling. Many of the criticisms white Americans have made about different races, for example, are in fact true in great part. Not necessarily because this is how they should be or how they have to be but because we have made them true. Many of us see a high number of black people and Hispanics as criminals, as gangsters, and as thieves. We see Native Americans as lazy drunks who only want to take free money from our government and live on welfare. We see Asian people as those who want to use our own economic situation against us. And more recently, we see Middle Easterners as fanatical terrorists who only want to kill us. There are so many cases we can cite to prove this. We have no reason to doubt it. "It's true!" we say.

JEFFREY B. BRANDT

Racism happens to be one of the most twisted or unnatural manifestations of prophecy that exists. Here in America, racism thrives although it is considered very taboo on a public level. One can hardly mention the word without causing conflict of some sort. Racism often manifests in the form of anger, although it is truly based in fear. Where fear exists, we often cover it with anger as a form of psychic shield.

When we say it's true, what we don't seem able to see is the just-as-real fact that it is we who have created the scenario that has basically forced so many of them to be so. We have molded and killed the ambition that so many "colored" people might have to adjust to a society that will not allow them to participate at the same level and manner "noncolored" people might participate. We have created our own worst enemy so to speak.

After being hit on the head with all of the hype about supposed equality, many who would like to decide we can live the same are let down by the very people they tried to help. For this reason, many then decide to publicly speak of equality while they secretly believe (and manifest) just the opposite. They come up with the excuse to have the problem groups justify their worth while they do everything possible to deny them the chance to do just that, even if this sabotage is on an unconscious level.

Racism is a very large problem for humanity. Attacking this problem or even trying to understand it better will not resolve it. All sides of the issue have their reasons and a great deal of truth. If resolution is the goal, we need to focus on correcting the error of our own manifestation, our own thinking.

Understand that the human brain is the most incredible tool that has ever existed. The capacity we have to manifest our future is, for all practical purposes, unlimited. It doesn't matter in the least where we are at the present moment. Nothing in our world can interfere with this capacity. Our reality doesn't matter because our reality is only an illusion that we have created. The only thing that stands between where we are and where we want to be are the limitations we place upon ourselves through a perception of a reality we decide is real. Welcome to the world of paradigms.

Our brain is like a genie. It will perform wonders in our quest to create whatever reality we may ask of it. The problem then is that we have never really understood exactly how this genie functions. Most people rarely realize what they are truly asking for.

Will vs. Imagination

The messages we send to our computer are, for the most part, very inconsistent, even contradictory. We will one message while we imagine something completely different. In this case, the imagination will win because imagination is the key ingredient to manifesting any reality. Look to any creative example, and you will see not stagnation but growth. Everything begins with imagination, without exception. We have accomplished with our imagination what was supposedly impossible.

We light our night skies. We heat and cool our homes, enabling us to live anywhere on this planet. We fly through the air and into space. We reach the bottom of the seas and come back, dry. We travel around the world and communicate from any place to our home, instantly. Yet, after all of this, we still can't seem to get along with our fellow living beings. It all comes down to a distorted view of these beings in relation to our world. We see a world full of conflict (caused by "them"), and a world full of conflict is what we continue to manifest. We reap the seeds we sow.

The brain will work toward the achievement of any goal we set for it. It will only be a matter of time before this goal is manifested. How much time it requires depends on our consistency and conviction more than any other factors. Here is where we talk of perseverance and faith in our religions. Our ability to manifest functions perfectly. We are living what we have created and will continue to do so. In propagating a world in which control and manipulation are the norms, we will be controlled and manipulated. In taking from our world without consideration for the rest, we are taken from without consideration. The Bible said, "Do unto others as you would have them do unto you." This little phrase carries a lot of weight with respect to how we experience our world.

We decide not to let the world get us down, and we make every effort to get others before they get us. Surely, we will experience a surmounting stress that will eventually get the best of us. This is because with a philosophy like this, our imagination is clearly in conflict with our will. We will a prosperous world for ourselves while we imagine it being a hostile world, and a hostile world is precisely what we will experience.

It is in facing seemingly insurmountable obstacles that we tend to look toward religion. I read somewhere that it is when the ground seems to be slipping out from beneath our feet that we tend to look to the sky. This is because somewhere inside of us that little voice of intuition, which is always with us, begins to be heard in our desperate search for solutions to the increasingly hopeless situation we feel we are in.

Many have reported a moment of divine enlightenment in passing through these dark times. When all seemed to be lost, they gave up their souls to find peace within themselves. They say they were touched by a universal wisdom that gave them a new direction to walk or some interpretation of the same. What this really comes down to is they gave up their will and any further expectations for their future. They decided, at last, to let things be as they are. In doing so, they were touched by an inner peace that can only come from letting go. They experienced the essence of how we can be at any time if we can only learn to let go of what is out there and live by what we, in truth, are.

CLOSE YOUR EYES TO FIND YOUR WAY

We are to experience this life in any aspect we choose. We decide if it will be a pleasant experience or otherwise. The key is the same for any man, for any religion, for any philosophy of self-help or personal improvement. Let go of the will to control, imagine your world as you want it to be, and live this experience. This is not just positive thinking. It goes beyond this. We must really imagine this as our reality. The moment we try to impose our image of how things ought to be upon another individual, we are, in essence, denying our faith in that our world is as we want it to be. Our message becomes contradictory.

This computer we have inside our head is an extremely sensitive instrument. It will pick up on this contradiction the moment our will and imagination go separate ways. It will go with what we imagine, not with what we will, as it always does. This is all it can do. It does not have the capacity to decipher anything but what we imagine. For this reason, it is vital that we be clear in our programming of this computer. What we think and feel on the inside really is more important than what we preach or how we act. It is our inner world that truly matters. So how do we assure the message we are sending is the message we really want to be sending?

Clarity of thought is the answer. This is where the ritual of religion may be most helpful. The concept of prayer basically comes down to a moment of clear or uncluttered consciousness for the purpose of setting us on the correct path toward our own desired realization. The same can be said for any relaxation techniques such as yoga, meditation, or self-hypnosis. Positive thought can definitely be of aid to us as well as daily affirmations and any number of other techniques we may find from a variety of sources that deal with achieving our goals in life.

In any case, we must realize that we, and only we, are responsible for how we interpret our present situation. No other holds the key to our paradise, and we hold no other key to paradise than our own. We can help others in the way of showing them a better way, but only they can make the decision to manifest a better situation for themselves.

On Wisdom

I look at the world. I see that it is so wrong, but I see no reason not to be strong. I feel the love that is all around us. I sense the wisdom that it is all OK. The knowledge is indisputable proof that the world is not as it should be. Neither for me nor for any other individual that shares in this thing we call life. The knowledge is there for all to see, but knowledge holds no answer. Alone, it is not the key. Knowledge is but a mirror of our outward expression.

The only truth to seeking a path in the promise of a better future lies in letting go of the knowledge, to surrender ourselves to the continuity of wisdom, which embraces all things the same. From this point, we truly become consumed in our world. And knowledge becomes an intricate part of our being.

Chapter VIII

LIFE DIVERSITY

Life. It is different for each, and yet it is the same for all. Our lives are like snowflakes. Each one is unique. You may compare our lives to the spots on a leopard, the fingerprints on your hand, a grain of sand, or to the leaves of any tree. Diversity is everywhere. Diversity is the standard. This is another lesson life has to offer us. Everything is different, and yet it is the same. This is the way it always has been, and it is the way it should be. Life is not static. It continues as an eternal dance. This dance continues to change as well. We call this evolution. It is the most natural condition of life and one that requires no force whatsoever. Beyond not requiring force of any kind, there is no force that will stop it. It is as eternal as life itself and will continue so long as life exists. It is life itself.

Every child comes into this world, a naked expression of this diversity of life. This expression is perfect in every respect. It is perfect as it is. There is nothing lacking in this expression of perfection. Nothing we may do could possibly improve upon this expression of life. The best you can do for a child is learn from him or her. Understand the child really is the teacher, and we adults are the students. At least this is the way it should be until we learn what we have forgotten.

JEFFREY B. BRANDT

How much do we rediscover about ourselves when we have a child? Any parent who takes his or her job seriously knows what I am talking about. You can read all the books you want on the subject of raising a child. But until you have a child, you do not know how to raise a child. In raising a child, we are reminded of our own life experiences. For example, we may be reminded of seeing something for the first time and the excitement that accompanies this experience. The pure wonder of innocent observation is stimulating to the spirit as well as to the mind. This plays a beneficial role in the developing character, and it is something we tend to let go of as we grow. This is life education. It is the essence of life, to grow and to prosper.

Another point about life and evolution is although it may not be stopped, it can indeed be influenced to a point. In fact, it is influenced by us in many ways. We have, perhaps, altered the course of life's evolution in countless ways since we began our effort to control our world. We have created numerous breeds of animals that may never have existed without human intervention. Many new plants or hybrids could also be said to be manmade. This brings us to another valuable lesson: only the essence of life's continuance seems to be a golden rule. How that life manifests itself may be completely open to new ideas as life's power to manifest itself in new form is unlimited.

With all of the diversity that exists, we must recognize the force that maintains this diversity. This force is called balance. We have only recently begun to consider this force that has been around for as long as life. We call the study of this force ecology. It is when we upset this balance that it sorely makes its presence known. We cannot destroy this force because it is one of the primordial forces of life. We can only alter the structure of the diversity that exists. Whatever we may do to affect the balance is only temporary. Soon afterward, it will correct itself. Although the resulting structure may be quite noticeably different than it was previous to the intervention.

In any case, we need not concern ourselves with the world. The world will continue in one form or another. It is how we affect the life force, of which we are a part, that we should concern ourselves. Whatever we do to the world, we are in reality only doing to ourselves. The condition of our world is a good indicator of how much (or how little) we venerate ourselves. What we have done to ourselves thus far is a far cry from being venerable.

Life is something greater than any individual component of it. There is only one life. We are each expressions of this, and each expression is unique. The key to finding harmony in our life is found in the acceptance of all its diversity. How much conflict did we create in our attempt to limit this diversity or in judging one form over another? What we attempt to destroy tends to come back at us with a vengeance, although not always in the same form. Very often, this vengeance multiplies in its undesirability for us. What we attempt to control will usually end up controlling us. This encompasses everything from natural plagues to social problems.

As far as social problems are concerned, most of them were created by ignoring life's need for unique expression. We all too often offer only negative attention to the eccentricities that surge from truly free and unique individuals. We try to inhibit their free spirit by forcing them to conform to some ideal we have decided was ideal for all because it suits our limited manner of viewing the world. The world is far greater than any man will ever realize.

Laws seem to be the most logical answer to any problem. The real problem is our not knowing what the problem truly is. Our logic in the case of controlling completely natural human behavior has not always considered the motivation for it but rather the manifestations of what we have decided were problems. This logic is the same with what might induce someone to place his finger in the hole of a leaking dam. The river will flow. It is only in its nature to do so, and an alternative escape will be found. Eventually, we will have the river finding a completely unnatural course to accomplish the only task it knows to do. Flow. An unobstructed river levels itself and poses no great threat when given the space it needs throughout its natural cycle. Create a dam to obstruct this flow, and you create a potential disaster of gargantuan proportions.

In the natural world, there is a concept we call the law of the jungle or survival of the fittest. This law assures the continuing prosperity of any given species for an undetermined time. This law exists within our human dominion as well, although that which we regard as the fittest has become quite distorted. Brute force or straight-up intelligence have little to do with one's ability to thrive or even to survive well in our non-natural realm. We have created such a labyrinth of misrepresented laws that do more to dissuade worthy growth and prosperity than they do to diminish any real detriment to our society. These laws have staled candid creativity. Our creativity has become more measured as more laws come into place.

Laws, in essence, are not made to protect but to control; and control is a force that leads to distortion of thought. In effect, these laws have permitted and even encouraged the rise of truly twisted ideologies within humanity. They are the number one force driving us to widen the gap between humanity and the rest of the natural world. Our lives are becoming more unnatural with each succeeding generation. We are the only species with so many homicidal tendencies, problems with addictions, sadomasochistic and sexual perversions, etc., all seemingly by nature. This is not nature.

We have gotten to the point where we don't seem to understand anymore what is or isn't truly natural behavior. Plotting against others, sexual attraction to people of the same gender, unprovoked aggression, substance abuse, and many other behaviors have all become more or less accepted as being normal while something as natural as sexual attraction for a budding young girl and nudity in general have become taboo in most societies.

Even the desire to delve into a career by unconventional means is not accepted. Here, I am referring to those gifted individuals with a desire to advance a society's capacity in a certain area. Those who would only be limited by following the accepted norm of studying that career in a university just so they may receive a title or a certificate from someone (who may very well be less enlightened in the subject) saying they are qualified.

This unnatural inhibition of totally natural tendencies or desires is often the cause of serious problems. First, these problems develop in individuals. Later they develop within society in general. Just take a good look at the number of delinquencies today's societies have related to sexual conduct or drug abuse and compare this to all of the laws we have in place. These laws supposedly counter this deviation from what we consider to be proper conduct. You will see a direct correlation between the amount of restriction and existing delinquency. And the forms of this deviation continue to become greater and even more perverted. We are living in an increasingly dangerous society.

Besides being outright dangerous, our world is becoming less pleasant in many forms. Confusion is rampant, causing a terrible depression in the masses. It seems to be the ones who most want to do the right thing in their lives who are becoming victimized with increasing frequency. This is a direct result of our encouraging a predator society by way of attempting to exert control upon our world. Everybody seems to be searching for something more, and they want it yesterday. More and more, we see what is available to us; and we like what we see.

For this, we owe thanks in great part to the media. The media is a powerful tool. The extension of our means of communication has reached to nearly all parts of our planet. This can be a great benefit to us, but it can also be our downfall the moment we give it more weight than we give our own thoughts, feelings, and conjectures. We must not lose sight of the fact that all we see on the media came from the mind of another individual whose views are as subjective as our own. Use the media as a source, but it is not the only source. And as an external source, it is not as relevant to you as what comes from within.

Much of the confusion we are experiencing today is because of having access to so much conflicting information. We can find any opinion we may want and evidence to back that opinion up. We see so much of the world and others' experiences that we are depending less on our own life experience. Conflicting information is to be expected when dealing with so many different sources. Keep this in mind and take lightly what is said. We each have ideas. Children are most comfortable with their own ideas. It is in growing up that we begin to depend more on others for our information and, sadly, for our opinions.

This is natural because of the need to work or perform certain tasks in life. The trouble is we tend to take this to the extreme by looking to others for answers to questions of the heart. Asking for and getting advice is one thing. But in making the final decision, we must realize it is our heart. And it is only our decision. We have what we need to answer questions of the heart. All we need to do is listen to our heart. Let another help you to hear what your heart says, but don't allow that person to tell you what your heart is telling you.

Understand there is knowledge, and there is wisdom. They are not the same thing. Knowledge is a product of the mind. Use your mind in dealing with information. Wisdom is strictly a product of the heart. Use your heart accordingly. Western societies have long given up using the heart to depend more on the mind, in general. Only the philosophers and grandmothers have maintained the prior alive to any great degree. In the Eastern cultures, you will find more of a tendency toward the use of the heart over the mind.

It is interesting to note that the Eastern cultures are coming to depend more on the mind while the Western cultures are beginning to orient themselves more with the heart. The reason becomes more obvious when one steps back to see that the East is becoming more modernized in a material way while the West is beginning to fall into decadence from its relative lack of exercising moral behavior in favor of living in excess.

Can we see the lesson in this? Diversity! Academics are fine so long as they treat only the academic world. This is not real life. Academics has little relevance to real life other than as a theoretical basis to grow from. Remember this. Questions of the heart don't belong under the jurisdiction of the classroom other than in an analytical form. As we find in the study of sociology for example. Living a materialistic life is not a bad thing so long as we don't place too much focus on it, neglecting the wisdom that must go together with the knowledge. Teachers would do well to keep the following in mind:

> The best thing you can teach the student inside the classroom is how to think for him or herself outside of the classroom.

We are all teachers. We become a teacher the moment we begin to express ourselves. Be careful what we teach, that we don't propagate confusion but clarity of thought. We do this through sharing ourselves without imposing our will upon others. We are only an expression of the infinite wisdom that exists, and each expression is unique. This is the way it should be.

Chapter IX

DREAMING

> The quality and quantity of our dreams
> is exactly reflected in
> the quality of our lives.

Life begins with a dream. Dreaming is the most natural thing for a young child to do. We are born with an innate ability to dream. Every great idea has its beginnings in a dream. As life goes on, we tend to be discouraged from allowing ourselves to spend too much time in this state. Why? Because we were told it is not productive. Try telling this to any artist of great works, a writer, or an inventor. Try telling this to an entrepreneur or a leader. Dreams are the visions of what may come. They are the windows to our future. They are optimism in its essence.

Allow yourself to dream. If you are young and dreaming is still a large part of your daily life, be grateful. Enjoy this phenomenon. Exploit it with every opportunity you have and develop it. If you are one of the many who consider themselves to have outgrown this activity, step back from your life for a moment and examine it to see it for what it really is. Are you happy? Dreaming is the best you can do whether you're nine or ninety. Dreaming is the key to sustained health and youth.

Dreams, like everything in life, seem to be cyclical. A dream precedes creation. From the dream, an idea surges. Ideas are opportunities. If we act on these opportunities, we create. With every act of creation, there is an explosion of energy. Ask any musician, writer, or inventor. He or she will tell you these moments are the most intense moments of life. There is an indescribable satisfaction that comes with experiencing something new. Our interest is sparked, and we begin using this newfound energy. As we assimilate what is new, we begin to feel comfortable in this new level of existence; and the energy begins once again to dissipate. As the energy dissipates, we begin to dream anew. And the cycle repeats.

This cycle is the same as that for eating, drinking, breathing, or sleeping. We need to eat, drink, breathe, and sleep. We also need to dream. Each of these cycles, of which there are seven, expresses a different level of the vibration of life. What follows is an explanation of the ascending order of these vibratory cycles.

The seven levels of vibration:

Existence

I see existence, as it is for us, as a vibratory state that is not something to be ignored or even to be taken lightly. We are conscious beings, unlike a rock that cannot contemplate its existence. It simply is. We are conscious, and we are curious. We are the same as all living creatures in this respect. The plant grows toward the light. A dog arranges a comfortable place to lie down. We are present in more than just the physical world. We are all aware of our world of thought. We dwell in these worlds simultaneously.

It is important to understand the importance of maintaining an awareness of our thoughts. Our thoughts are what control our essential state of being. Two people may have the exact same physical experience while they experience it in completely different ways. Understand this is a choice.

> Life may be trivial, but
> how we choose to live it is not.

Eating

Eating is the most basic vibratory state after mere existence. It is the most physical of them all. It is communion with the earth as much as is mere existence. This is the basis of sustaining physical existence. How well one eats is clearly reflected in his or her body. Everything we consume is filled with vital energy. The better the food, the higher is its vibratory nature. Raw fruits and vegetables vibrate at the highest levels while processed foods vibrate at much lower levels.

The simplest rule of thumb to remember in deciding what to eat is to think about which form is closer to its most natural state. Raw fruits and vegetables are better than frozen. Frozen is far better than canned. Canned is better than imitation.

Drinking

Next comes drinking. Water is fluid and promotes fluency of life as it animates us. Again, it is wise to consider the more natural form as being the better. Plain water is better, by far, than the many sugary juices available in the market. Bottled water is usually much better than tap water. Distilled water is better than normal bottled water. And the natural water we find in raw fruit and vegetables is the best of all.

Breathing

Breathing connects the physical with the spiritual. This is the force that transforms our experiences. Think about how proper breathing can alleviate fear, depression, or anger. During an exam, breathing well can help us to recall information. Very important to being able to breathe well is to focus on our posture. Proper posture facilitates the mechanics of breathing. Stretching our muscles often will ensure the oxygen we breathe reaches its destination to do its work.

Sleeping

Next is the vibration of sleep. This is what clears the mind, and sleep promotes synchronicity of body and mind. It is in this state that our brain works to organize our experiences of the day. Proper sleep is what helps to keep us sane and gives us the ability to solve our problems. Good sleep habits are also vital to maintaining our immunity to physical sickness as well as cure whatever managed to get us in the way of illness or injury.

Dreaming

Dreaming is the state of vibration where everything new begins. Inspiration finds a home in dreaming. Inspiration is the force of optimism. It is the force to go on to better things. This is what makes life worth living. Frustrate this inspiration, and you kill the life force within the creative type. It is for this reason suicide and insanity rates are higher in people who thrive on creativity: artists, musicians, writers, and the like. This would include those who are lonely and are only dreaming of finding a significant other. Dreaming is only one step away from Holy Communion.

Holy Communion

Holy Communion is a direct connection with the greatest creative force of all, that which we may refer to as God. In this state of vibration, there are no surprises and no questions. Everything we experience in this state is accepted as it is. Everything is known. We recognize the oneness we are with the world. It is the most comfortable state of existence we may know. This is the goal of the yogi, the philosopher, and the saint. It is also a state that every soul has experienced at one time or another. Although usually this state lasts only an instant, it can have a profound impact on our view of the world. It even changes the course of our lives. Without exception, this view is one of peace and calm.

Dreaming is synonymous with imagination. You will remember that imagination is the language of the mind. And it is the mind we use to manifest our world. Children dream of a different kind of world while adults settle for and try to hold on to the one we have. The elderly long for the world they knew, that of the past, the way things were. The world continues along at its pace and changes with each generation. We choose where we want to be within this cycle.

Time is but an illusion of convenience for us. It is only a perspective. The real world knows nothing of time. The real world can be had in an instant if we can only learn to imagine. We use time as our excuse to delay that which we are afraid to imagine or haven't yet learned to imagine. We use time to give in to the dreams of others; and we live their world, not ours.

Don't be afraid to imagine. Don't be afraid to dream of a better world. And most importantly, don't be afraid to take action and live this better world that you alone can create. Live it well that you may be the example for others to see that dreams are the seeds of our experience. If the fruit you bear is beautiful and sweet, you will find others willing to share in the harvest; and your garden will extend. Remember, the more you give to others, the more you, yourself, become.

Dreams and Memories

Time is what we feel when our memories exceed our dreams. The moment we allow this to happen is the moment we grow old. We cease to feed our dreams and begin to feed upon our memories. Our memories become finite the moment we stop striving for our dreams. When our dreams die, our memories will soon fade.

Don't stop dreaming. And don't stop reaching for those dreams. Keep the fire burning on into the night. The harder the wood, the hotter is the flame. There are far more uses for a hotter flame.

Chapter X

SUCCESS

Basically, success can be summed up as achieving what we set out to achieve. In a certain sense then, we are all successful. Although what we set out to achieve is not always what we really want to achieve, it is what we imagine ourselves achieving.

The fact is we can actually have what we want. It really comes down to understanding how to get it, not whether we can get it. Furthermore, it doesn't seem that anything is definitely impossible. How in the world would you convince any person two hundred years ago that we would be flying around the world and into space, or seeing real-time images from any place on the planet by watching a small box, or communicating with anyone, anywhere, using a cell phone? For as commonplace as these devices may seem today, they are all miracles from another perspective.

These are all rather material in essence, but we can look to other types of miracles as well. Look at what people have done with nothing more than their own lives and words. There were Gautama Siddhartha, Jesus Christ, Mahatma Gandhi, Confucius, Lao Tzu, Mohammad, Martin Luther, and countless others whose ideas or manners have changed our world.

Common people have had relatively simple ideas that completely changed our world. The best example of this may be Johannes Gutenberg, who is generally accepted to have invented the movable type printing press. He was a simple man who probably never realized the impact he would have on the world.

Others, perhaps, knew the impact they would have and had set out to do what they did for just that very reason. We have people who came from extreme poverty to immense wealth in relatively short periods. Some examples are Oprah Winfrey with her talk show, the Jackson family with their music, Kim Woo Chong with Daewoo Industries, Colonel Sanders with Kentucky Fried Chicken, etc.

I could go on and on with examples of success, but the point I am trying to make here is simple. Examples are everywhere of ordinary people making an effort to succeed and achieving that dream. It has been happening for a long time and will continue to happen. If one really wants to make it big, that person can begin by doing the most natural thing; that is, to say the most natural thing for those who have achieved success. One must believe in one's self. Ultimately, successful people don't follow. They lead. It is kind of like the saying about the sled dogs: If you're not the lead dog, the view never changes. Wouldn't we all like to be the lead dog?

The reality is that opportunities abound more today than ever before in history. This is only obvious when you look at how diverse our lives have become. Just look at the choices one has today with careers, for example. With all of these choices, we see more and more people who say they want to be successful. But they don't have a clue as to what they want to be successful at. This comes back to the premise of ignoring the world and listening to your heart. Your heart has no doubt about what your mission is here, and everybody does have a mission. You will never hear what your heart has to say while you are too busy listening to what the world is rambling on about. Step back and get to know yourself. Leave your social life behind for a while. Don't listen to your friends, or your family, or your dog. Be simple. Be alone.

Many of the early cultures knew the value of being alone at a certain age. The Lakota (Sioux) had their ritual of manhood where a boy who was coming of age would be sent to stay on a hilltop for a few days. He was given no food or water. He was made to suffer alone, to search and find himself and his path in life. This was good, as it gave that boy an opportunity to reflect upon his spirit without the interference of others. Later, he would relate his experience to the medicine man who would then help him to interpret the message.

Artists, musicians, writers, inventors, and other creative types thrive on being alone. Ideas don't surge from groups. They can only come from the individual. The accepted tool of brainstorming to solve problems, so common in engineering circles today, is used to come up with any number of ideas and to find a connection between ideas that will function as a solution. Still, it is the individual who comes up with each idea. Brainstorming is used to create raw material (ideas), which comes from individuals, in mass quantities. This raw material is then analyzed by the group to find a viable answer, which ultimately comes from an individual and may be further developed by other individuals. In any case, it is the individual that is responsible for any specific progress that is made by the group.

The same goes for the learning process. Others can give you ideas or explain concepts, but still it is your mind that must understand and either accept or reject those ideas or explanations. In this manner, we understand that success can only come from within. Connect with the world as an extended part of yourself. The answers you seek are all there within you. Here is where you find all you need. It is imperative that you learn to rely upon yourself to find success. No other may give you success; and by the same token, no other may hinder your success.

Remember, it is your imagination that holds the key to your life experience, not your will. And your desire is a neutral tool you use to feed the imagination. Fear is the most prominent obstacle standing in the way of synchronizing our imagination with our will. It is fear that keeps many of us from achieving that which we believe we want. It is a fear that stems from our unwillingness to accept full responsibility for our current situation. This fear can be overcome through understanding the role we play in our worldly experience. This may not be an easy lesson to assimilate as we remain fearful creatures.

If we are not experiencing that which we believe we want to experience, it is a sign that we are not ready to accept ourselves or our present experience. We don't yet understand ourselves. We need to grow in our own right. We can use the lessons of others, but they will mean nothing to us until we assimilate them. They need to become a part of our programming. This often requires a great deal of repetition. Our imagination and programming were built on repetition. Mostly, this is done on an unconscious level throughout our lives. This is our programming at work. There is nothing that maintains this programming other than continual feedback, whether it is internal or external in origin.

Internal feedback is the only feedback that is real to us. It consists of the messages we send to ourselves, whether consciously or otherwise. On a conscious level, we can easily control our internal feedback. It is on an unconscious level that we have a more difficult time in controlling this feedback. Our mind carries on an incessant conversation with itself that we are rarely even aware of. This is a rather simple fact to prove if one would take just a minute to attempt to control one's thoughts. Take a minute right now, and try to maintain only one thought in your mind within that minute. Only one minute. You will quickly realize this seemingly simple task is something nearly, if not completely, impossible for you.

From this little experiment, you can see just how much activity goes on in your mind on an unconscious level. Imagine the number of thoughts that pass through your mind in a day, a month, a year. Imagine the number of thoughts that have passed through your mind during the course of your lifetime that you were not even aware of. You will have noticed also that in observing this little conversation your mind was having during that minute of observation, there was a lot of repetition going on. The unconscious mind loves to repeat thoughts like a child who is learning loves to repeat the same experience again and again and again.

Now think about how many negative comments you have heard related to the chances of achieving success that which you believe you want. Multiply the number of times you have heard those comments by the gazillion times you have probably repeated them on an unconscious level, and you will get an idea of how imbedded those negative comments have become and how they have managed to control your imagination.

If this sounds overwhelmingly fatalistic, relax. All is not as hopeless as it seems. The human brain is an amazing tool. Programming can be changed. It is not static. It constantly evolves and creates new realities, as this is in its nature to do. External feedback is only as relevant as we allow it to be. This is why we must, as any successful person has done, learn to reject the status quo in our own existence. We must learn to trust our own instincts. We need to create our own system of feedback that is not so influenced by that which is external to us.

Controlling the external feedback we receive is something that is usually out of our control, but controlling what we accept and what we reject is perfectly doable. The more challenging part is controlling that internal feedback derived from the incessant conversation our mind carries on with itself. This can be a process that we begin to control slowly at first and with more ease as we begin to build upon more positive reflections of our life experience.

This is where time spent alone can be vital. We may need to isolate ourselves from the external as much as possible, at least in the beginning, until we learn to depend less on the comments of others. If we feel we need some external influence, we can depend on the many books, tapes, or videos that deal with the topic of self-help or achieving the goals we set.

What is of vital importance in our learning process, be it from books, tapes, videos, or merely dwelling in thought, is that each lesson must be learned not once but many times. Keep in mind, repetition is the key. You can increase the effect of this repetition by choosing multiple sources that lead to the same conclusion but offer different perspectives of the same. What I mean to say is by getting different perspectives or ideas concerning how to achieve what we want in life, we begin to make connections between these different sources. Making connections between two apparently distinct ideas is the key to exponential or accelerated learning.

An example of this is reading several books on self-improvement written by different authors or even from different categories. Try reading some that give very straightforward, scientific advice. Then try reading a fiction book or two that treat the theme of self-improvement. Finally, you could maybe even try a book or two with more of an esoteric or religious presentation, even if this is something you wouldn't normally read. The idea is that you will notice some common threads between the different teachings. When your brain makes these connections, the concepts will become reinforced in your psyche, your programming.

You may have noticed much of this book says the same thing in different chapters as well. That is OK because each chapter has its own way of saying the same message: Let the world go, and focus only on yourself.

This repetition acts to feed our evolution. Our perspective of the world begins to change. We gain conscious control over our reaction to this world. Eventually, we even begin to see how we affect our circumstances in life. The sense of adventure that was so much a part of our childhood outlook on life becomes ours once again. This is recuperated energy of our youth. It is very exciting to feel growth, even more so after years of stagnation. Life really is as interesting as we make it.

Immersing ourselves in the world of the natural can be most inspirational as well. If you are not accustomed to walking in the natural environment, begin without looking for anything in particular. Soon you will find much to catch your curiosity. Give in to your curiosity, and take in all you can without judging. This is much easier to do if you are alone. If you must have company, let it be a dog. You will learn much from this companion, but don't interact with him or her. Rather, allow yourself to observe this wise one as you observe the rest of this natural world. Reignite the spark of the child that still exists within you.

This will not only help you to relax and feel good, but you will also find some of the most valuable lessons life has to offer from these experiences. Getting close to nature is the fastest way to get close to ourselves. We begin to see our role in this world as a mere observer. We learn that things don't need to be judged, only to be accepted. They are a part of the way things have always been and always will be, regardless of what we may do to try to change them. We learn to respect all that is, including ourselves. We learn to see the primordial love that exists in all things natural. We see more clearly the falseness and irrelevance of what we had accepted as the total of reality before. We will have expanded our paradigm of reality.

This is what makes our journey home more accessible. In the ultimate sense, we may find the triviality of our desire to achieve so much. We may realize that we are just fine the way we are. But if this is not the case and we still want more, we will find our journey more acceptable as we learn the destination is not as important as the journey itself. Enjoy the journey. Don't worry about when, or even if, you arrive at your destination. Nobody arrives at success anyway. It is a journey or a path that one may follow, and it does not ever end.

> Curiosity is a wonderful form of reverence toward creation.
> It is nothing more than a show of respect for something
> greater than oneself.

Most important on this journey toward your idea of success is that you show compassion toward yourself in the form of patience. Remember, the journey is the destination. Growth is the essential purpose of living. As long as we are growing, we are living. And nobody reaches the peak of any mountain without first facing and then overcoming an upward climb. Even a mountain doesn't forever remain a mountain. And finally, a mountain only appears as a mountain while it stands before you. Good luck on your journey, and carry with you always a smile.

The Key to Success

The key to success lies in the intensity in which you apply yourself to whatever you do. In short, you must be what you are trying to accomplish, and you must live it every moment of your life in every aspect. It goes beyond simply believing in yourself. It means accepting the simple truth that you are what you are, and that is what you will always be no matter what may happen around you. With this frame of mind, there is no room for self-doubt. And for true success, there can be no doubt.

Chapter XI

SUFFERING

I suffer because from this suffering I find the purest form of love, peace, and self-acceptance. I knew this all along, but I didn't know exactly what it was that I knew. I only knew that I was on to something beautiful, and that this something was like nothing I could ever find outside of myself. It was only in myself that I confided. I am only now beginning to realize why, and it is something I genuinely appreciate.

I know not yet where my journey will lead me. But I feel secure in that I am accompanied by all that is, and that nothing lacks on this journey. I walk it humbly, and I share myself with any soul. I offer myself without resistance, and I find that nothing is taken from me. Rather, I myself become a part of all that have received a part of me. In essence, it is in giving that we grow, not the contrary. When we realize this is when we realize the truth: Greed makes lesser people.

Live for yourself. And you will be living for the world, and you will receive everything. If you live for the world, you will be living only for yourself. And you will receive nothing. We are one, and it is when we realize this that we will be free. There will be no conflict between us.

It is not for us to question the reasoning behind the truth, only to accept it for what it is. We cannot understand it without being a part of it. If we must question something, let it be our deviance from this truth, for herein lies the source of all conflict. Conflict is only internal to us. It is only in our interpretation that we find it. The world of which we are a part is pure and immune to conflict. There exists nothing less than perfection. Let everything be. Focus only on yourself, and you too will suffer. If you can accept this suffering without the slightest denial, you will experience a dissipation of this suffering. You too will find the purest form of love, peace, and self-acceptance. This is essential baptism.

Life Is a Pool of Water

> Truth can be found at the bottom of this pool. The more you disturb the water around you, the more distorted the truth appears. Remain still, and let life be as it is naturally. The truth will make itself known to you although you are only floating on the surface.

Be an eccentric. Be in love with life and love to experience what few ever have. Learning new things is the payment received for investing in new experiences. New experiences bring growth. Thrive on growth because growth keeps an active mind. An active mind is an open mind. An open mind is the best tool to have in overcoming obstacles. It breaks paradigms, and breaking paradigms to overcome obstacles is the surest way to feel good. With experience often comes suffering, but we need to see this suffering as that which helps us to appreciate what we have been through. There is great satisfaction in this view of suffering. Don't fear the pain of suffering, but don't seek it either. Accept it as it comes and know that within it lies another lesson. Life is the lesson. Learn it well. You might feel good, even as you are suffering.

Equally important to personal growth is seeking the opportunity to share your growth, your experience, with others. This is, perhaps, the greatest gift you can give to others; and giving is the best expression of your being alive. Give everything of yourself without reserve. You can never run out. The more of yourself you give to others, the more you become. A part of you is carried on in all whose lives you have touched, both now and in generations to come. Remember this when you are dealing with others. Always give the very best of yourself.

As giving to others is important, acceptance of others must be included. The world is full of individuals. Each individual is another world in the making. Grant each person the sovereignty to be his or herself. This is the true meaning of giving. As our world is revealed to us in its own time, so is the reality of every other individual. You cannot make a flower bloom before its time, and you cannot keep that flower from blooming without killing it. We are all on a journey made unique for each one of us. This is where it all comes back to having an open mind. Do not judge. Keep your mind open, and keep on growing in your own right. Finally, keep on sharing yourself, but with acceptance of those whose experiences are still different from your own.

Suffering is not a good thing but neither is it as bad as we may believe. It is a part of life. This part of life is something I don't believe any person has been able to completely avoid. The amount of suffering seems to be related in some way to how intensely we relate to the essence of life or how intensely we are searching for that essence. Those who have suffered the most in history have also been blessed with having custody of an internal peace that is nothing less than enviable. What these souls have left behind has been noted as pure love, and they have given us hope for a better life. We look to these people for inspiration.

On the contrary, those who seem to have suffered little personally tend to leave behind a legacy of torment and shame. There seems to be nothing enviable in their ways other than the temporary power many of them had experienced before their fall. It is easy to see the internal conflict they experienced along with this false power, even more so toward the end of their reign.

The majority of us fall between these two extremes. We will neither experience great personal struggle leading to a profound peace nor will we seem to fall into a life of inborn power that ends with disgrace. We live our mundane lives very superficially—without risks, with no threat of great loss, and no chance for significant personal growth. Is this a bad thing? I doubt that it is. If one experiences no calling, that one is content to simply be. Period. For some, perhaps, unknown reason, that person is not yet ready for this journey of self-search.

If one is to receive a calling, he or she will be made aware of this calling in the proper time. Like a flower opening up, we can do nothing to change this timing. It seems the moment one receives this calling is the moment one begins to truly suffer. Like birth itself, this passage is a difficult one. We are in the hands of something greater than we can fathom, and we must trust this something with our lives. Death, as well, is often preceded by something painful. This pain is temporary; and with its conclusion, we will not be the same. Growing up and leaving our home behind can bring with it its own kind of pain. We accept this pain as we know there lies greater opportunities beyond.

The whole of life is based on transition. And as with any transition, comes something given up to receive something new. Understand this. Suffering really comes down to our attachment to that which we must let go. It is the sense of blockage of that which must be let to flow. Life is fluid.

> Where do I go now that the child has grown, and no more fear remains? This is the question that comes to mind. In life, I have given more than anyone will ever know. To the people who know me, I am happy, though they know not how I can be so.

Although suffering itself may not be something we can avoid, our interpretation of that suffering is something we will always have control of if we so choose. This control comes in facing ourselves and resisting not what happens in the world. We observe the world without judgment and continue working on ourselves. Look to new experiences not as a loss of old ones; we only add to our repertoire of experiences. We are here to grow, and this means seeking a certain kind of uncertainty which is inherent in anything unknown. The result of any new experience holds promise. Even if the result is not what we desired, it holds wisdom that we can use ourselves and share with others.

Be bold in your decisions, and be humble in your present stance. There will always be more to learn in following any path. Just be sure that path is the path your heart suggests, and you will never go wrong. Trust in your divine intuition, and whatever suffering you do experience will undoubtedly lead you to the freedom you seek.

Welcome to My Water

> The deeper the water, the slower one must walk through it. At a certain depth, we can no longer even walk. We must

make the total commitment to dive in and swim or avoid it all together but how much we miss if we choose not to swim. Water can be most refreshing, even more so when our journey has been an arduous one.

The deserts of life are many, and the chance for a refreshing swim are few and sometimes far between. Don't fear the water for it is life. Without it, we will surely die. So the next time you come across it, whether it be a stream, a pond, a river, or sea, don't hesitate to experience it in all of its depth. Take the plunge. You will emerge a new person, clean, refreshed, and ready to go on in your journey of life.

Chapter XII

THE KEY: THE POWER OF ENERGY

Freedom is the ability to act rather than react. Acting is the essence of creation. It is a genesis. We are meant to be creative creatures. No true creation has bad intent. It can only move us forward. Creation born of the energy of reaction is the only form that can stall our advancement. It is the application of energy to stifle another energy that is always negative.

Reaction has a necessary place as a survival mechanism. This means it is necessary when there is a threat, real or potential, to the physical being. If your hand comes into contact with an extremely hot object, you react, even before your mind has time to consider the situation. This is a real threat to your physical being.

If you are walking down the street and you suddenly hear the loud screech of car tires braking directly behind you, you react, even before your mind has time to consider the situation. This is a potential threat to your physical being.

When reaction does not fulfill a need to protect us from threat to our physical being, real or potential, it may be considered a conditioned reaction. Another way of saying this is it may be a habit.

JEFFREY B. BRANDT

Many authorities agree that 90 percent of our behavior is driven by habit. Habit, in itself, is not necessarily a bad thing. It serves a very valuable purpose. Consider how many routine and daily activities we go through basically on autopilot. We get out of bed, walk to the bathroom, clean our face, brush our teeth, get dressed, make breakfast, and drive to work. Many of our tasks at work as well are basically automatic. They don't require our conscious attention to perform.

Habits can make our lives much simpler, for sure. The problem arises when our habits are actually not serving us in the best form. When habits actually cost us energy or well-being yet we still feel compelled to carry them out, I consider them to be addictive. The mind is extremely prone to addiction. In particular, the ego is all about maintaining the status quo. That is to say, the ego is always trying to keep us within our comfort zone.

When we consider addictive habits, we predominantly consider the habits of smoking, overdrinking, poor eating, gambling, drug use, etc. What most will admit, but few truly consider, are the habits of our attitudes. This means how quickly we anger, our slothfulness, our tendency to view the negative side of life's affairs, etc.

Our attitudes are truly habitual in nature; thus, it may be considered addictive. Scientifically, this may be arguable. However, trying to change a standing attitude may prove to be as challenging as trying to kick a chemical habit. Trying to control or eliminate a chemical habit causes our mind to send us messages that interfere with our intended goal. "You've done so well at quitting smoking. You've proven you can do it. You deserve to have just one more before quitting for good. Go ahead, just have one more before calling it quits for good."

With trying to change an attitude habit, we face pretty much the same dilemma. "Here you are trying so hard not to explode with anger, and just look at the way the people around you are behaving. I swear they're either trying to taunt you or they're just plain stupid. God, don't they have any idea that they really are the cause of your being angry all the time. You've got the right to really explode this time, just to let them know how you feel. Go ahead. They deserve to hear your true feelings. Make them feel bad."

It has been said, "Habits are like a comfortable chair, easy to get into and hard to get out of." In a certain sense, we may have a more difficult time with changing our attitude habits simply because we don't consider them to be addictive. Because of this, we are not prepared to face our goal of overcoming them in the same manner we would with a chemical addiction.

Having read this far into this book, you should probably have no doubt accepting the oneness between the body, the mind, and the spirit. There really is no separation between these three aspects of our being. When it comes to fighting a chemical addiction, most tend to fight this addiction on all three levels. That is to say, we fight these addictions on a mental or spiritual level as well as on the physical level. We present ourselves to counseling and education most readily with the treatment of a physical addiction.

This same three-pronged approach should be applied when we decide to change an attitude. This is where many have failed to find success in their attempts at changing an attitude habit. They limit their strategies to those of an intellectual nature while they ignore what they could be doing on a physical or spiritual level. Often, that which we perform on a physical level can be more effective than our simple awareness or attention to a problem attitude we are trying to modify.

To get a better grasp on the subject, it may be beneficial to understand the role of energy and its blockage on our ability to function free from addiction.

Energy

Energy is meant to flow. It must be able to flow freely to avoid certain undesirable conditions within our being. Put another way, the more we can do to free up the flow of energy within our being, the easier any task becomes. This includes the tasks of regaining health, overcoming addiction, or modifying our behavior.

It can be helpful to first understand the relationship energy blockage has with different maladies. Energy can be blocked on different levels of our being. Exactly where this blockage takes place and just how long it lasts determines the malady we suffer as a result. Take a look at the following diagram to better understand.

Energy Blockage

Level	Acute Result	Chronic Result
Physical	Fatigue/pain	Disease
Mental	Frustration	Resentment
Emotional	Anxiety	Depression
Spiritual	Indifference	Cynicism

Consider this chart a skeletal structure. As you can see, it can go much further in detail. Frustration could be anger. Resentment could be hate, which could be based on feelings of guilt or of personal inadequacy. It would be easy to make this far more complicated. However, doing so would not necessarily make it equally more helpful. Suffice to understand how a blockage in one area can, and usually does, affect other areas.

For example, physical blockage creates fatigue. Physical fatigue can frustrate us mentally, making us more prone to anger. This is stressful, which can cause disease. Disease can bring on depression, which can destroy us spiritually. We may then become cynical.

It is important to remember what was said earlier:

- Energy is meant to flow.
- Any blockage of energy will have a negative result.
- Any release of blocked energy will have a positive result.

So what can we learn from this? Anything you can do to free up the flow of energy in any area of your life will positively affect every aspect of your life. Free up the flow of energy, and you get better results in whatever you endeavor. Now, look back at the chart. You will notice that there are basically four levels where blockage of energy may occur.

- Physical
- Mental
- Emotional
- Spiritual

We will take a more detailed look at each of these four areas. First, we will take a look at how we may free up the blockage in each. Then we will see how we may accelerate the actual flow of energy. Keep in mind that many of these suggestions will benefit us in more than one way. As was said earlier, freeing up energy in one area will ultimately benefit every area.

Physical: Cleanse To Release, Shock To Ignite

Our physical body becomes dirty, and we clean it. We have no doubt about how much better we feel after coming out of the shower. We feel clean and fresh, and this feels good. What most people don't consider, however, is how the inside of our body becomes as a result of what we put into it.

Diet is a subject I could go on and on about, but I'm not going to go much into it for two reasons. First of all, it would be way beyond the scope of this book. Secondly, I could hear the "experts" now, screaming about my lack of credentials concerning said matter. So let me just say this: We can benefit greatly by taking the same course of action within our bodies as we do without.

Much of what we eat and drink is not at all beneficial to our well-being. Much of what we eat is actually quite damaging. Many people have even lost touch with their natural ability to judge what is or is not beneficial to their bodies. Many more may be aware that much of what goes into their bodies is not beneficial; but, for one reason or another, they don't really give much importance to the thought of what they are doing to themselves through their diet.

How far one wishes to take internal cleansing is entirely personal. It may depend upon how open-minded one is or just how desperately the need is felt. If you feel so inclined, I would recommend you look into colonic cleansing. If you are looking for high impact, this will definitely give you what you're looking for. To varying degrees of intensity, there are the many herbal cleansing programs available for you to look into.

If you're not so inclined, I would recommend, at the very least, to look into a change toward a more natural diet. Raw fruits and vegetables are the perfect foods for flushing out and maintaining our digestive tracts clean and responsive.

Having a clean body both within and without will inspire greater energy levels. Beyond eating well, we should consider drinking plenty of clean, pure water and breathing fresh air as well.

Our bodies are designed to move. This seems to be something only too obvious. However, we tend to give the concept far less importance than it deserves. There was a time when exercise was unheard of. Life itself was full of movement and resistance. With the advent of recent technologies, our lives are becoming more and more sedentary. It was only the most recent generations that have begun to put focus in the idea of exercise to supplement what little movement our present lifestyles require.

With exercise, as with cleansing, how far one wishes to take it is entirely a personal decision. When it comes to increasing our energy levels, stretching or yoga-type exercises may be the most beneficial. To greatly increase the effectiveness of these, adding some aerobic exercises will do wonders.

You don't necessarily need to follow some set routine with stretching unless you are called to get more involved. Simply being aware of your body when you are spending a great deal of time being sedentary and breaking this up with some type of movement can be extremely beneficial.

For example, when watching TV, get up and move during commercials. Stretch your toes away from you then toward you while you are just sitting there. Stretch your arms above your head for a few seconds, and then let them rest beside you. Pull your shoulders back as you breathe in, and then relax as you exhale. The idea is to connect with your body and experience in your mind what your body is telling you. This becomes very easy when we move in a focused way.

As for breathing, this activity in itself can be an excellent form of exercise. First thing in the morning, before even getting out of bed, spend a minute taking in a few deep breaths to fill your body with oxygen to begin your day with energy and delight.

The same breathing exercise can be used when you get into bed at night to release the tension of the day. Give thanks that your day is done, and you may now sleep without immediate concerns. This will help you to relax and fall into a more restful sleep. Be sure to smile while doing your breathing exercises.

Many of our daily activities can become opportunities to connect with our bodies. When taking a shower, be sure to really be aware of how the warm water feels on your skin. Imagine how it is opening up the pores to release the toxins from within your body. Breathe the moist air, and feel how it soothes your throat and lungs. Enjoy the melting tension in your muscles as it leaves your body and gets washed down the drain.

And be sure to turn the water cold just before getting out of the shower. Enjoy the exhilarating shock for a few moments. This will surely give you a jump start. The body likes to be shocked once in a while. This change of stimulus to the body can instantly inspire increased flow of energy and feelings of well-being.

If you stub your toe or bump your shin, take a moment to enjoy the excruciating pain of the moment. Know that this pain will be short-lived. The pain will be less severe; and although not planned, you can take advantage of this moment as it is definitely a shock to the body. Allow the flow of energy to surge.

When climbing a flight of stairs, decide to take two steps at a time rather than one. As you take each step, feel the muscles in your legs and enjoy the added stress. If you feel yourself breathing heavier than usual upon reaching the top of the stairs, consciously take in a deeper than normal breath, and then let it out with a sigh of accomplishment. Be happy.

Mental: Clear To Receive, Stimulate To Grow

Like with a cluttered desk, it is equally difficult to accomplish much with a cluttered mind. We are generally assaulted with roughly fifty thousand thoughts during our every day. To accomplish most anything of importance, it is imperative that we be able to focus. This is especially true in the area of creation and growth. Creative energy comes only through a clear and focused mind.

To clear the mind is to release the noise of unguarded thought. In short, it means to focus our awareness. We accomplish this by submerging our consciousness to the depths of our present experience, whatever that experience may be.

Giving your mind something definite to hold on to is the surest way to bring focus to your thoughts. This can be accomplished using any number of techniques. One of the simplest techniques may be to focus on our breathing. If your mind is unusually noisy at the moment, you may begin by lightly stretching first. Begin by taking a deep breath in. During each stretch, concentrate on exhaling long and slow. Hold the stretch while you take a slow, deep breath in. While breathing in, feel how this stretches your muscles even more. Then, exhale again as you return to a more relaxed position. Once relaxed, you may find it sufficient to simply focus on the breathing while further relaxing your body.

Once your consciousness has sunk to a sufficiently deep level, you may move your attention to the task at hand without losing focus. This technique is excellent for writing, drawing, composing music, or solving a problem. Even before reading to learn, this preliminary activity will greatly increase your powers of retention.

In this relaxed state of mind, we are prepared to receive inspiration from the ether of the universe. Whatever we are to do, we can do so with augmented sensitivity. This is a state of mental bliss. Even doing nothing at all can be a rewarding experience. From here, we can easily raise our being to a more spiritual level.

This exercise of quieting the mind is something that can be most beneficial to us when practiced on a daily basis. Our modern lives are basically replete with stress. A break of even a few minutes can help us to cope for the entire day if we only plant this objective within our psyche before allowing ourselves to return to the outside world.

Your mind is designed to grow. This requires stimulation, just as a muscle needs to be stimulated to grow. Reading may be one of the best methods to stimulate the mind. Other ways may include watching videos, listening to recordings, or simply observing our world.

EMOTIONAL: EXPRESS TO RELEASE, INSPIRE TO ATTRACT

Emotion is the energy we transmit to the world. This energy, as all energy, has a range of frequencies. The higher the frequency, the more liberating is the energy we transmit. There is no more liberating emotion than the emotion of love. This is because the emotion of love vibrates at the highest levels. The equally opposite emotion, fear, is the least liberating of all the emotions. The simplest way of determining the frequency you are experiencing or transmitting is to consider just how liberated you feel.

Emotion is an energy we generate on our own. Only we are responsible for the frequency we generate. However, the frequency we tend to generate is often influenced by the frequency we receive from the ether, from others. This is because the energy of emotion is reciprocal in nature. It tends to attract that which vibrates at the same frequency as itself.

If I give you a thought, say, the Statue of Liberty, you will think about the Statue of Liberty. You cannot avoid it. You will undoubtedly add something to the thought as well. You may add an image of the Statue of

Liberty. Perhaps, you will even add the green color to your image, adding details I didn't mention. Once I stop talking about the Statue of Liberty, you have the choice to continue thinking about it, or you may choose to think about something else.

The same thing happens with emotions. If you walk into a room full of emotion, you will undoubtedly pick up on the predominate feeling. You will more than just sense it. You will be drawn to generate the same feeling. If the energy of the room is of the same frequency you are generating at the time you enter, you will feel very comfortable being there. You will feel that you fit in.

If the energy in the room is of a higher frequency than you are generating at the time you enter, you will sense an urge to raise the frequency of your own energy. You will feel more liberated if you follow through. If you try to resist and maintain your energy at the same lower frequency, you will sense a certain level of anxiety. This is because in your attempt to maintain your energy at a lower frequency, you are, in fact, blocking the flow of your own energy.

If the energy in the room is of a lower frequency than you are generating at the time you enter, you will sense this as well. Here you have the choice of how you will react. You may choose to lower your frequency, leave the room, or maintain your higher frequency.

Sometimes people choose to lower their frequency to blend in. Even though in doing so they are synchronizing their energy with the lower energy of the room, they will feel a sense of anxiety. This is not healthy as it is blockage.

The second choice is to leave the room. In this case, you may still feel a certain sense of anxiety as a part of you is aware of the lower energy you are leaving behind. It is kind of like entering a swimming pool and then getting out. You come out of the water, but you are still wet. Of course, once you get away from that environment, you may find it easy enough to bring yourself back to the higher frequency you were experiencing before you arrived.

The third choice is to remain in the room but maintain your same frequency of energy. This may prove to be a bit of a challenge as your simple awareness of the lower frequency that surrounds you does tend to impact you. You may feel somewhat out of place as you feel something trying to bring you down to match what is around you. If you manage to maintain your frequency, you will surely find others, those nearest to you, at least feeling the urge to accelerate their own frequency to match yours. If not, they will quickly move away from you to find someone more in tune with their own frequency.

There is another choice you can make that may be the ideal choice for two reasons. That other choice is to use the situation to accelerate your own frequency. First of all, accelerating your own frequency is always the best thing for you. You will feel more liberated. Secondly, as was stated earlier, the energy of emotion is reciprocal. The higher your frequency becomes, the more powerful of an influence you become to those around you. They will not only pick up on your higher frequency, but they will pick up that it is actually accelerating. This will draw them to you more than it will repel them away from you.

This is because a part of us has a predisposition to feeling more liberated. Simply put, it feels better than the alternative. But how does one use a negative situation to actually feel better? The answer is in gratitude! That's right. As you walk into a room where the prevailing frequency is much lower than what you were experiencing just prior to entering the room, take a moment to really feel grateful that you are not experiencing that same level of energy. Rejoice.

There is magic in feeling genuine gratitude. It ranks right up there close to love in frequency. In fact, gratitude is actually an expression of love. Vibrating at this frequency, our energy becomes a magnetic force that draws to us more of the same. This means you feel better, and those around you have the opportunity to feel better. Those who do begin to feel better then make it easier for even more to come around. Then you will truly have something worth celebrating.

Gratitude is the key to increasing the vibratory nature of emotional energy. This is important because when you increase the frequency, you increase the magnetic quality, the attractive force to bring good into your life.

Spiritual: Become Aware, Give Thanks

To be spiritual is to be aware of the energy that is you. This is only possible in the here and the now. Not to be confused with the mere results of the use of this energy but to understand you are the creation, the process, and the result. You are the good, the bad, and everything in between. You are in everything, and everything is in you. You are both the observer and the observed.

The blockage of spiritual energy then is to sense one as somehow separate. You sense that you are apart from the world, from others, or from the different levels of your being. In observation, you sit in judgment. And you are able to criticize. Only in this state can we be indifferent. Only in this state can we become cynical.

Life can be a challenge, when we are drawn to superficial ideals on an almost nonstop basis. Our world—the world we have created—is almost entirely superficial in its makeup. Prolonged exposure to our typical modern lifestyle can drain our batteries, whether physically, mentally, emotionally, or spiritually. The way to recharge our batteries is to find a way to step back from the superficial lifestyle for a time. We need to submerge to the depths of ourselves, to distance our focus from the surface of what can seem a stormy sea.

To accomplish this, we need to physically isolate ourselves from the modern world as much as is possible. If you live near a natural area, you are fortunate. I believe getting close to nature is, by far, the best way to recharge. If this is not possible, find a quiet place to be alone while you practice the exercises put forth earlier in this chapter, in the sections on physical and mental energy.

In the section on emotional energy, we learned about the power inherent to gratitude. This is truly a spiritual emotion. It can have the most profound impact when conjured up during a meditative state. As are all emotions, gratitude is reciprocal. When you use gratitude, it is as much a gift to you as it is to what you are feeling grateful for.

Live your life to the ideals of this chapter as much as you can, and your life will change dramatically. Keep in mind it is a journey. Be kind and forgiving of yourself. Always begin wherever you are and know that it is getting better. This makes gratitude easier to express. Becoming a better person is always rewarding, even in unexpected ways. Keep your emotional energy on the highest frequencies.

Chapter XIII

THE JOURNEY

The vastness of the human spirit far surpasses that of the physical universe, which is itself infinite in nature. This physical universe is but one aspect of our total sphere. It is only that (perception) which has thus far been manifested. Our perception goes far beyond what is manifested. We may create in our mind that which does not yet exist in the physical. Beyond perceiving these imaginary things, we have within our ability to create them. It is this ability that expresses the divinity which we are. This is our true nature. In expressing this true nature, our world can only be a beautiful journey.

I am all for seeing the big picture in every aspect of or action we take in life. It is important to first realize this is not a journey to some other place. It is a journey of a different sort. You see, you have already arrived. Proof of this is in the fact that you are reading this book. If you had not yet arrived, you would not have been drawn into this book sufficiently to have read this far. You would have found this book to be irrelevant or too far out there for your liking. Truly, you've always been here. Your journey then is in discovering this wonderful place in which you already are in.

Consider a beautiful sculpture. Before the artist begins his work, he has but a large block of apparently unimpressive stone. From this stone, he begins to chisel away until what he has envisioned begins to reveal itself in a way the world can appreciate. He has added nothing to the stone. He has only removed what he saw as unnecessary material.

The same is what you do on your journey to self-discovery—you remove the falseness of your being, the confusion, and the error to reveal the truest sense of yourself. Your truest self is not about your life's daily, mundane experiences. It is not about your schooling, your career, your activities, or simple interests. It is about who you truly are. This true self is someone you may discover only through deep, pensive observation. You discover your true self through those meditative moments when you are alone without pressing activities. You see your true self when you are passing time in nature. You are revealed to yourself by reading a profound book on human nature. You recognize your true self while listening to a great teacher of life talking of the most esteemed qualities of human beings.

This book was written to be of aid to you on your journey to self. Although this book does contain all you will need to find your way to a more enlightened life—it is complete—I urge you to continue seeking out other books and sources always to broaden your understanding of every aspect of life. For this is the essence of life, to grow and to prosper.

Each of us is on our own unique journey. Each book, for example, has just the unique perspective of life as the writer had observed and experienced. It is almost as if the writer had actually written the book for him or herself. There is a certain truth to this statement. Therefore, it is likely that certain parts may ring true and relevant while other parts miss our sincere appreciation. This is not a bad thing, only evidence of the uniqueness of the individual.

My personal inspiration for what I write comes almost entirely from my life experience. Experience, I believe, is the best source of wisdom and understanding. Although reading had been a large part of my life always, I found nothing in a similar vein to my thoughts and observations until several years after I had written this book. I discovered the law of attraction, which I then learned to use to bring into my awareness some of the most profound writers I believe have ever existed. Reading the books by these writers was almost a scary experience for me. Previously, I truly believed my book to be nothing less than unique in its content. Beyond the content, I had never seen a book that spoke with such candor my perspective of the truth.

The first book I drew to me through conscious use of the law of attraction was Eckhart Tolle's *The Power of Now* (New World Library). Next, I came to know two other writers' works from nearly a century earlier. Robert Collier's *The Secret of the Ages* (Tarcher Penguin), and Prentice Mulford's *Thoughts Are Things* (Barnes & Noble). Robert Collier and Prentice Mulford's books really struck a chord in me. I no longer felt that I was writing in the vein of virgin territory. I was amazed that these books had been around for so long yet were so little known.

The idea of self-discovery is all about seeking our potential to find peace within. Prentice Mulford said something that I feel is the wisest of advice, "Never in thought acknowledge an impossibility." I would like to add a little of my own idea to this statement: Always in thought acknowledge the possibility. Feed the possibility your unfettered imagination until it grows into a probability. Apply your intention to this probability to bring it into reality for you. This is the essence of how to make an impossible dream a reality.

JEFFREY B. BRANDT

One of the most difficult aspects of being on the journey to personal enlightenment is that we are trying to find peace in a world that appears to be so full of suffering. Almost from the onset of this search, we feel a certain struggle between the world we see that can be (the possibility) and the world we actually do see—our perception of reality. It can be frustrating to read the words of the enlightened teachers when they speak of how perfect everything is when our daily lives are fraught with conflict. Try as we might to maintain a sense of inner peace, we find we are assaulted from every side of our daily lives by what can only be a plot to destroy our every hope for attaining that peace.

This is where I hope that this book may be of a different sort of help. The primary focus in seeking enlightenment is on the self, yet we still need to coexist with a world that in so many ways seems to be going in direct contradiction to our desired direction. What this book tries to be so candid in its expression about is that it is perfectly normal to see the reality of the world for what it appears, even if what we see does seem to be in conflict with the ideals of spiritual growth. The ideals so eloquently expressed by the spiritual teachers really can be had by any individual who sincerely seeks them, in spite of the apparent state of affairs of the world at large.

I believe the world will reach a state of divine enlightenment someday. However, I don't see this happening any time soon. In fact, I see that things may even become far worse than we might imagine at present before this happens. It may very well be many more generations before this world comes around to common acceptance of the truth. However, this doesn't have to mean a thing to the individual who has a sincere desire to open up to a more divine way of life at this or at any time. It is a journey only the individual can embark upon in any case. Furthermore, the more individuals who arrive, the more others will see the light of possibility in their own potential.

Eventually, becoming enlightened may be the most natural outcome in any given lifetime. If this is not the case at present however, you need not concern yourself.

There is something very important to consider when you are drawn to observe your life situation or the world in general. In observing your life or the world as it is, you may experience more of a sense of lack than of fulfillment. This can bring much pain to your being. Understand that what you are observing does not have to be your experience. Your focus in observing the way things are is on the outside; leave the effect of this observation on the outside as well. Use the observation to educate yourself as to how not to place your own focus. Examples abound to show you that trying to control the outside world brings nothing more than dissatisfaction and even pain.

If your intention is to better your life situation, you must maintain your focus on the result of your quest. Obviously, what you see around you is not your desired result. Or you would not be on a quest in any case. Focus only upon that which you desire for yourself, and experience within your being that which you would feel if it were real for you in the moment. Looking back from this point to where you actually are will help you to see what your next step will be to move closer to your desired result. This is how we may move forward.

This line of thought is the key to making our journey easier in that we must keep an open mind to possibilities always. It is fine to acknowledge what we see as reality, but this doesn't mean we need to give credence to it. What is important is that we not dwell on the deficiencies we observe in our world but place our focus on the possibilities and on the growth we make personally. This is what is meant by letting the world go on.

You will notice on your journey that there will be times when you may feel extremely depressed, and other times you may feel almost pure ecstasy. Take the hint to realize where your thoughts are focused during each of these extremes. Understand the message that can be found in how you are feeling.

When you are feeling most depressed, your focus is on the way things are. You are dwelling in thought on your life experience, on what you see around you. You are observing what you consider to be validation of your suffering. This does not feel good. You may feel trapped and controlled. You may believe in that moment that you are at the mercy of the universe.

This is when your inner self is trying to give you the message that your focus needs to change. So long as your focus remains on observing your situation, you will continue to feel bad.

When you are feeling inspired, your focus is on the possibilities available to you. It is possible to feel this way even when your current situation may be considered very depressing. Think about the times when you were feeling down and of a certain moment you were touched by an enlightened thought. You found a way out of your suffering. Your situation in that moment may not appear any different to anyone observing from the outside, but the focus of your thoughts has changed.

Once your focus has changed, your feeling good is the message sent from your inner self that you are now on the right path to manifesting the change you desire. Acknowledge this, give thanks, and be alert for inspired thought that will surely come to guide you. Trust inspired thought and act upon it immediately. Inspired thought will always be thought that brings with it good feelings.

Your job is to allow appreciation, gratitude, and inner peace into your life. You cultivate appreciation by being willing to help others in their own journeys. You cultivate gratitude by expressing thanks for every little thing that comes into your life, focusing on the good in everything. And you cultivate inner peace by accepting whatever pain you feel as a loving message that there is a lesson to be learned in your present situation (what you are focusing on in thought). Do not judge, ask with an open mind for assistance, and wait with faith that the answer is only waiting for you to notice it.

I see no end to this journey. For now, the primary goal seems to be simply living in peace for most. I see no reason for sickness, hurt, or even death. Life really can be all that we imagine it can when we learn to understand ourselves. I believe there will come a time when we will realize this.

In Conclusion

In this book, you will have noticed a single underlying message that was repeated throughout, although each time in different form or from a different angle. This is the way of our lives. We continue to receive the same message, a very simple message, until we, at last, take that message in. We have all that we need within. Nothing out there needs to be controlled by us. It is only when we realize this that we can free ourselves from whatever misery we have created for ourselves.

When in doubt, return to the here and the now, and observe without judgment. Answers are to be found by quietly taking in others, the self, children, books, and nature. Spend time in the natural world. Silently observe and spiritually connect with the animals, the plants, the rocks, and the sky. Remember also to note how they all come together to form the scenery.

Learn to love life, and enjoy the diversity that exists. Keep a humble view of yourself, and look to grow with every opportunity. Welcome to my water, and I hope that you will welcome me to yours. My journey is not yet finished, and I am continually interested in expanding my world. I hope you have enjoyed walking with me on this facet of our journey. Remember, we are all teachers; but none is higher than the one who comes next.

It is every teacher's dream to impact a student, but sometimes it is the student who impacts the teacher.

Finally, I would like to leave you with some inspiring words I wrote, lying in my bunk, while stationed at Fort Irwin, California, back in January 1982. I called it "The Four Truths," and it has served to guide me well on several occasions in my life.

The Four Truths

The first truth is history. Know your past, both of the individual and of the cosmos. From this, you grasp concept. Concept is an open-minded pattern of thought that separates you from the ignorant who struggle with detail. History of the individual is of one's self on a spiritual level or of mankind as a whole. History of the cosmos is on a divine level of reality and of time.

The second truth is prophecy. Know your path, both of the individual and of the cosmos. From this, you grasp control. Control is the discipline that separates you from the lost who walk aimlessly through life knowing not what it is that they seek. We need a sense of direction to survive. Prophecy of the individual is of one's spiritual path, where an individual is going (evolving). Prophecy of the cosmos is of the energies of the universe where everything is being guided through this void.

The third truth is religion. Know your purpose, both of the individual and of the cosmos. From this, you grasp stability.

Stability is the strength that separates you from the weak who do not own their mind nor do they own their body. We need to be stable to be consistent and, thus, grow. Religion of the individual is to know what one is doing here and now. Religion of the cosmos is something on a very high order, of which there are no words to explain. Thus, to fully understand this truth, you must bring yourself upward toward the gods.

The fourth and final truth is success. Know your potential, both of the individual and of the cosmos. From this, you grasp inspiration. Inspiration is the light that separates you from the blind who see not the path to follow. We need to see a way in order to truly grow. Success is, perhaps, crude in the eyes of one who is not human. However, this is a most vital truth to obtain if one is to keep in touch with the realities of this world, lest he be lost in his own fantasy, never to find his way back to reality. Success of the individual is knowing your full potential as a human in your worldly environment. Always keep in mind, this world is very real and is necessary. And you will not be lost. Success of the cosmos is the boundless, unlimited potential of all that is. There are no ends or final steps.

With the understanding of these four truths separating you from the falseness of the world yet keeping you in touch with the reality of this world, you may ride a parallel path to the ways of the world in a most intimate way. And yet, you may remain pure of sickness and of guilt, the symptoms of sin. Have a most honest relationship with others, with yourself, and with God. You will not be overcome by the temptations of Satan, for Satan relies on lies and trickery. A lie can only be seen as truth when one is disillusioned by an inconsistency or a filter. It is your responsibility to remain consciously alert to catch these inconsistencies and to reject them if they will create a filter. We can only hope to catch every one; however, by practicing to be observant, we cannot help but to improve ourselves. Use no filters, only absorb. Answer nothing, only wonder.

I do not teach, but rather I learn, experience, and become in truth, myself. Who am I to teach of the truth when it exists everywhere? Each moment I would spend in teaching others, I would waste a moment I could be learning myself. You may believe this to be selfish, but I do not judge. If one is to experience the truth, he must see it! He cannot see it through my words, lest he experience the life within those words. You may look through me as through a window but do not see me. See the truth. When you look through a window, do you see the glass? Do you look beyond to see what is revealed by the glass? I am only the glass.

THE END

Index

A

addictions 48, 84, 110-12
   chemical 111

B

balance 82
beauty 58
brain 77, 100
brainstorming 97
breathing 92, 116

C

celibacy 58-9
child 65-73, 81-2, 99, 101, 107
church 40, 42, 47, 49-50, 58
Collier, Robert 125
   Secret of the Ages, The 125
competition 69, 71
cultures
   of Christianity 18
   of the East 86-7
   of the West 18, 44, 58, 61, 69, 87
curiosity 102

D

destiny 46, 49
diversity 81-3, 87

dreaming 89-90, 93
drinking 92

E

eating 91
Eden, Garden of 29
ego 39-40, 70, 110
emotions 118-19
energy 16, 33, 90-1, 109-14, 116, 118-21, 132
   blockage of 112-13
   frequencies of 118-21
existence 90

F

feedback 98-9

G

gratitude 120-2, 128
growth 102, 104-5

H

habits 109-11
   attitude 110-11
   chemical 110
history 40, 49, 132
Holy Communion 93

I

imagination 77-9, 93, 98-9
inspiration 93, 133

K

knowledge 13, 80, 86-7

L

laws 83-5

M

messiahs 57-9
Mulford, Prentice 125
   Thoughts Are Things 125

P

person (enlightened) 60-1
Power of Now, The (Tolle) 125
Prentice Mulford 125
prophecy 75-6, 132

R

Racism 76
religion 50, 53-5, 132-3

S

savages 41-2
Secret of the Ages, The (Collier) 125
self-discovery 14-15, 124-5
sin 29, 37, 46-7, 64
sleep 92
stability 132-3
success 95-7, 102, 111, 133
suffering 15, 57, 103-7, 126, 128

T

Thoughts Are Things (Mulford) 125
Tolle, Eckhart 125
   Power of Now, The 125

V

vibration 90, 92-3
  levels of 90
violence 40-1, 43

W

wisdom 80, 86-7, 107, 125